What Others Say about Th

"It is possible that the greatest plague we have in our culture today is that we are a people of disquieted souls. This is the symptom of something lost within. When we reject the Transcendent, openly or subconsciously, we tumble into a stormy sea where nothing really satisfies; where nothing truly comforts. Like drowning beasts, we thrash about for anything to quiet our restless souls. In a world that makes it so very hard to 'be still and know that I am God,' . . . Lane Cohee's *The Disquieted Soul* may be just what the doctor ordered."

—**Dr. Del Tackett,** Truth Encounter Ministries
and founder of The Truth Project

"This book will rejuvenate your heart! Lane Cohee's writing is refreshingly insightful, offering epiphanies you'll appreciate for years to come. He presents engaging, real-life scenarios and a welcome path for quieting your soul and enriching your spirit. By the end you'll gladly include meditation as part of your daily walk with God. Don't be surprised if you pick up this book to read again and again."

—**David Sanford,** author, editor, and consultant

"I just finished Lane Cohee's work *The Disquieted Soul*. It was not just a compelling read; it read me. Like a trail guide on a winding mountain path, Lane led me on an honest trek through his own heart, but in the process I discovered my own 'demons of disquiet' and 'cruel masters.' Thankfully, Cohee did not leave me in that place but guided me to a practical and profound means of experiencing the quiet of the gospel. I highly recommend it."

—**Rev. Mike Osborne,** dean of students and director of
Field Education, Reformed Theological Seminary, Orlando, Florida;
pastor and author

"A helpful book for those struggling with a disquieted soul from the 'over' syndrome: over-performing and over-committing, usually because of over-worrying and over-analyzing from over-perfectionism. Dr. Cohee calls us to quiet our souls by changing the voice we hear and redirecting our gaze to God's truth—about ourselves and our circumstances."

—**Dr. Randy Richards,** provost and chief academic officer and professor of biblical studies at Palm Beach Atlantic University; lecturer, speaker, preacher, and author

"*The Disquieted Soul* is an honest, thoughtful, and convicting look at the reasons many Christians find little actual rest for their weary souls. It shines a light into the dark parts of the human heart and reveals things we don't want, but desperately need, to see. Then it provides a biblically faithful and refreshingly practical guide to experiencing genuine peace and spiritual recalibration. The laser accurate insights in this book offer real hope and help for Christians willing to apply the life-changing, soul-quieting, familiar truths of the gospel in a fresh way."

—**Rev. Matthew Ryman,** senior pastor, University Presbyterian Church, Orlando, Florida

"Having spent many years balancing my faith with the many demands of business executive and family roles, I know how easy it is for our souls to become 'noisy.' Through *The Disquieted Soul*, Lane Cohee offers a transformational view into our life's journey and hope for true spiritual triumph."

—**Connie Cooper Shepherd,** executive vice president for strategy and planning at Palm Beach Atlantic University and former industry senior executive

"The Disquieted Soul reads almost like a treasure map drawn by one who has spent time lost in the dark jungle of his own soul. It captures the right blend of theological, practical, and personal. Lane Cohee vividly describes the jungle ("Discovery") and then builds a usable map for fighting sin and growing in grace ("Deliverance"). He offers a gospel-saturated perspective, flavored with helpful personal examples and illustrations. If you struggle with the "Demons of Disquiet," this might be exactly the book you've been looking for."

—**Rev. Bryan Clark,** co-senior pastor,
Trinity Presbyterian Church, Bozeman, Montana

"When I first met Lane Cohee, he was in the middle of this journey he so transparently shares with us in this book. What a pleasure it has been to see his physical, spiritual, and relational transformation into the man he is today! He speaks with the voice of experience and hard-learned wisdom. To all of us who repeatedly feel like we are one step away from failing at what is most important in life, Lane offers clear insight into our underlying dysfunctions and a proven path to victory and joy. With *The Disquieted Soul,* Lane gives us a needed solution to our deepest needs."

—**Rev. Jerry Klemm,** senior pastor,
Covenant Church, Palm Bay, Florida

Chris—

THE
DISQUIETED
SOUL

Thank you for
your kind and
insightful counsel!!

— Lme

The Disquieted Soul

Copyright © 2019 by Lane Cohee

All rights reserved.

Published in the United States by Credo House Publishers,
a division of Credo Communications LLC, Grand Rapids, Michigan
credohousepublishers.com

All Scripture quotations, unless otherwise indicated, are from The Holy
Bible, New International Version., NIV. Copyright © 1973, 1978, 1984,
2011 by Biblica, Inc. Used by permission. All rights reserved worldwide.

ISBN: 978-1-625861-33-7

Cover and interior design by Frank Gutbrod
Cover image by Chuttersnap/Unsplash.com
Editing by Amanda Bird
Proofreading by Elizabeth Banks

Printed in the United States of America
First Edition

THE
DISQUIETED
SOUL

Paths of Discovery and Deliverance

LANE COHEE

credo
house publishers

ACKNOWLEDGMENTS

I am not an author by trade so I am extremely grateful to those who have journeyed the writing trails before me and were willing to share their expertise. David Sanford graciously coached me through various nooks and crannies of publishing and promotion. Amanda Bird's keen insights and recommendations provided invaluable improvements of my mechanics and message.

I am also deeply thankful to my friends and family members who set aside time from their busy lives to read early choppy incarnations of this book and offer their support.

Many people have provided the lessons I needed to write *The Disquieted Soul*. Some are quoted in the book. Others have endorsed it. Still others have been kind, quiet, and patient companions through my paths of discovery.

At the top of that list is my wife, Cheryl, who has patiently loved me through 32 years of my often disquieted journey and has never given up on finding a path of deliverance.

I am deeply indebted to you all.

CONTENTS

PREFACE

In early 2017 I defended my doctoral dissertation. The event was a landmark in my professional journey, integrating research from the academy with years of experience as a business leader. I'd graduated in record time and enjoyed a successful first career. I possessed many of the trappings that would suggest a prosperous life.

But as with many who are blessed with some achievement, there was another side to my story. My life was chaotic. I drank too much. I was in lousy physical condition. I was a mediocre father and a poor husband. For all my success as a provider, my closest personal relationships were a mess.

Not coincidentally I was in lousy spiritual condition as well. I'd committed myself to the Christian faith nearly 35 years before but was running on fumes. Like a middle-ager living in his high school glory days, spiritual progress was a distant memory. I could still talk a good game based on years of residual knowledge, but I was marking time. I'd been going through the motions for a long while.

I've listened to many Christian stories, and mine isn't unique. We get to mid-life and we become content and lazy. We rest on our spiritual laurels—past knowledge and past service. We learn to enjoy the creature comforts of this life way too much. We stop attending to our souls, instead keeping them anesthetized with everything this life has to offer.

But God wasn't finished with me. Bit by bit he began putting me back on the treadmill, dealing with my coping mechanisms, spiritual sloth, and addictions. Like most people hitting the gym for the first time in years, I often didn't want to go. But clarity and renewal slowly took form. And then, before my eyes, he took decades of thoughts, writings, and musings I'd cobbled together, and put them into one cohesive story.

The story of restoring a disquieted soul.

INTRODUCTION

Disquiet — a state of troubled restlessness, anxiousness, agitation, and unease

My soul, be quiet before God,
for from him comes my hope. (Psalm 62:5 ISV)

I once had a friend call me one of those "tortured souls." By that he meant I was clearly prone to overanalyze, over-worry, over-perform, and over-do. I was restless, impatient, discontented, and anxious. I was driven to perfectionistic extremes and addictive tendencies. Internal turbulence, disorder, and even recklessness were regular companions. Peace, stability, and harmony were not. My friend could as easily have called me one of those "disquieted souls." And the more I lived, the more I observed that I was not alone.

You may also fit the pattern of a disquieted soul. You may be running as fast as you can on the treadmill of life, trying to escape your own unhappiness. You may constantly hear a voice inside telling you that whatever you do isn't good enough. You may have trained yourself to believe that restless discontent is just part of your DNA. You may seem

3

to thrive on stress and busyness—perhaps associating them with success and self-importance.

If you resonate with this portrait, I've written this book for both of us. It is organized into two parts, as shown, forming the shape of a "V." The first six chapters of discovery take us downward, diagnosing the pathology and root of our souls' disquiet. The final six chapters of deliverance take us upward, identifying a path toward recovery and healing.

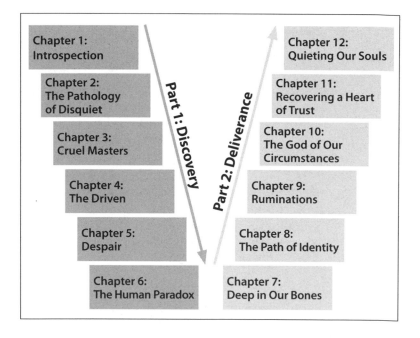

In this book I delve into some sensitive human behavioral topics with causes and treatments debated even amongst experts in the fields. As I state in chapter 5, more extreme cases of anxiety and depression can be chronic medical conditions with biological, environmental, and other contributors. I have attempted to neither over-spiritualize nor over-materialize these topics but rather to nurture a recovery involving both body and soul. I encourage anyone struggling deeply in these areas to seek out both physical and spiritual physicians. Ultimately, both body and soul were created by and for God himself.

Finally, I write this book from a distinctively Christian perspective. That may be attractive to some readers and unattractive to others. I only ask of each that if the path of discovery describes your human experience you give equal consideration to the path of deliverance.

"Lord, to whom shall we go? You have the words of eternal life." (John 6:68)

PART I
DISCOVERY

CHAPTER 1

INTROSPECTION

For as long as I can remember I have lived with a decidedly disquieted soul—a soul perpetually fueled by flames of anxiety and discontentment. Over the years I rarely gave it serious thought, assuming there were many more important matters in life. There are not. In my experience, nothing is more important to recognize and remedy because, left unchecked, a disquieted soul is spiritually suicidal by nature. *It ultimately charts a path of its own undoing.*

This statement probably sounds overly dramatic. After all, everyone deals with a little stress and dissatisfaction, and it's not quite the same as turning into an axe murderer or robbing a bank. Everybody gets a little restless and discontented with life—with their jobs, their circumstances, their spouses, and so on. Everybody wishes they made a little more money, got another promotion, or lived in a better neighborhood. Everybody can get obsessive, turn into a control freak, and find it hard to turn it off. Everybody can be overbearing, especially if they have a lot of demands and responsibilities. This is the world we live in.

I looked at my life this way for decades. I learned to look past my inability to calm my soul, even as I restlessly moved from one pursuit to another. The next job had to be done faster to meet self-imposed deadlines. Communication gadgets needed to be at the ready for fear of missing out. Every task required obsessive dedication so no one would find fault with my performance. I trained myself to disregard a heart that was always anxious, overdriven, and dissatisfied, increasingly operating in an anesthetized state and not truly understanding why.

Over the years I assumed this distressed state of being was simply a reflection of the way I was wired. It was, I told myself, part of my DNA, accompanied by a bit of youthful fidgeting. Since a disquieted soul is often relentlessly bent on achievement, I complimented myself for being driven. And since life often rewards those who are driven, I was happy to accept the accolades. In reality, it may have been partially true that "I was born that way." Personality studies indicate that some people enter this world naturally calmer and more tranquil than others. But for me and, I suspect, many like me, I was hiding behind something much more deep-rooted and destructive.

The Nature of a Disquieted Soul

A quieted soul is a contented soul. It is a soul at peace. Most of us have felt a bit of tranquil contentedness in life's happiest moments. We have experienced satisfied feelings—like a Christmas day when our children are playing, music is alive in the background, and all is right in the world. These are temporary glimpses and shadows.

But true quietness creates a much more powerful and lasting mosaic. For me the quieted soul is like a powerful yet calm river, its currents gliding as the rising sun charts a path overhead. The river is balanced and tranquil. It is serene and still. It is majestically at ease.

The quieted soul knows this balance and tranquility even in the midst of life's demands. The quieted soul is not motionless or passive. It moves with force, direction, and calling. It engages in the normal activities and pursuits of existence. It journeys through life's high and low tides. But it knows how to remain stable and at peace in their midst. The quieted soul lives within the disharmony of life but is not enslaved to that disharmony.

Conversely, the disquieted soul is like that same river in the midst of a torrential gale. Its waters are restless and turbulent. It churns and spills over the banks. It lives in a state of constant disturbance, buffeting everyone and everything that comes into its path. The disquieted soul is naturally driven to instability.

Shame and Pride

At first glance shame and pride seem to be strange bedfellows.[a] Shame hides while pride boasts. Shame feels inferior, while pride feels superior. Shame hears voices of disapproval while pride hears voices of applause. Shame defensively hides in the shadows. Pride bombastically parades in the streets. Ironically, shame and pride may start in opposite places, but they lead to the same destination. *Neither can see past itself.*

Because it is bred in varying degrees of shame and pride, the disquieted soul begins with a wrong view of itself. It instinctively places itself at the center of the universe. It engages in a perpetual battle to manage all its circumstances in the belief that it alone knows what is truly best. It cannot stand uncertainty because it trusts no one and nothing more than itself. The disquieted soul presumes godlike omniscience, demanding that life conform to its plans. And when life does not, it worries and rants, pouts and anesthetizes. In short, the disquieted soul is never satisfied nor calmed, because it always has to be in control.

Yet despite its natural position at the center of the universe, the disquieted soul constantly battles against the reality that the universe is too big for it to handle. Like a child trying to seat itself on a throne, the disquieted soul

---

a   Diagnosing shame and pride within ourselves is critical to the discovery process and addressed in more detail in appendix A.

vainly tries to occupy the place of God, all the while flailing in its human limitations. Hence it lives in a prison of its own making. It is a prison created by a soul constantly trying to be *superior* while constantly feeling *inferior*.

It's a prison created by a deformed sense of self—and a deformed sense of God.

Shades of Disquiet and Deliverance

To this point I have described quiet and disquiet in their extremes. In reality, of course, no soul lives consistently with both feet in one camp. Life is a composite. A soul may enjoy quiet harmony with God for a time, only to encounter extreme disquiet during another. These shifts might happen over a short period or even a single day. But some souls have a strong tendency to lean in one direction or another.

Everyone must do their own introspection, but I have written this book for those who look inside themselves and see—as I have—a strong propensity for disquiet. If you intimately feel the burden of restlessness, instability, anxiousness, and dissatisfaction, with a never-ending need to control your circumstances at any cost, I hope you find some keys to discovery and deliverance in this writing.

We may be assured that full deliverance for the disquieted soul will never come in this lifetime, because, in a strange way, the soul's disquiet ultimately stems from a haunting desire to recover paradise lost. Ironically, despite its frequent ugliness, the disquieted soul instinctively knows that a perfect lover, perfect peace, and perfect satisfaction truly exists, but it fails in its vain attempts to find them in this world. Many quote Augustine's confession, "Our hearts are restless until they rest in you."[3] But no heart finds complete rest this side of eternity.

Even on this side of the chasm I am certain we can do better than incessant disquiet. We can, as David tells us, learn to still and quiet our souls (Psalm 131:2). Such learning and training does not come through a "spiritual protein shake." Rather, it requires intense study and disciplining our thought lives in three crucial areas: the believer's true identity, God's true identity, and a true posture of trust.

That is where my journey is leading me—and perhaps you as well.

QUESTIONS FOR REFLECTION AND DISCUSSION

1. Consider the words and terms I have used to describe a disquieted soul. Also look up other synonyms for disquiet. Which of these words most describe you and why?

2. How would you define shame and pride? How do you see shame and pride operating in your life? Why do you think I suggest that shame and pride are the "parents" of disquiet?

CHAPTER 2

THE PATHOLOGY
OF DISQUIET

I f we seek to quiet our souls, we will get little help from this present world. We inhabit a culture that prizes—even glorifies—busyness and stress. While many of us bemoan that we are too busy, busyness is actually our modern badge of honor. One expert writes:

> This is success in America. Progress equals fast, which equals success, a recipe for addiction. Society is now dominated by beliefs, attitudes and ways of thinking that elevate the values of impulse, instant gratification and loss of control to first line actions and reactions. "I want it now!" or "Do it now!" are valued mantras for today's with-it person, young or old. Add to instant action the belief that there are no limits to human power, no limits to action, no limits to success. Fueled by the grandiosity and omnipotence of these beliefs, people get high on the

emotions of endless possibility with no need to ever stop or slow down.[1]

Rather than exploring ways to reduce our frenetic behaviors and their accompanying stress levels, we often appear intent on finding ways to *increase* them. Some experts have proposed that the psychological demand to never slow down actually comes from our underlying tendency to *equate busyness with importance.* That is, we derive psychological significance from a busy job, lifestyle, and task list. We crave the vicarious achievement of having successful children. These kinds of things, in turn, drive stressful activities and the associated stimuli that keep us addicted and coming back for more. It is a vicious cycle that one specialist attributes to a "reluctance to deal with ourselves on a deeper, more personal level." She states, "If we're dancing as fast as we can, then we don't have to think or get immersed in what's not being satisfied in our lives. . . . We're running away from our own unhappiness."[2]

Running away, of course, is the stuff all addictions are made of, and we are an increasingly addicted people. Our modern opioid epidemic has indiscriminately spread across an entire population, independent of social class or ethnicity. And while much attention has focused on prescription painkillers, one study shows the concurrent rate of alcohol dependency has risen 50 percent in just ten years. That study records that one in eight adult Americans is now considered an alcoholic.[3] Heroin use and accompanying deaths have tripled between 2003 and 2014.[4] Sex addictions impact an estimated 19.6 million Americans—as many as or more than those addicted to painkillers. And sex addictions tend not to fly solo, with 83 percent of self-identifying sex addicts reporting associated alcoholism, drug abuse, workaholism, or compulsive gambling.[5]

Behavioral addictions are equally or more pronounced among our younger generations. While every modern generation has grown up discussing the risks of drugs and alcohol, an entirely new set of process addictions is affecting teens today. These addictive patterns of repeated behavior take well-documented forms, like compulsive internet use and, in particular, gaming. But they also manifest themselves in gambling, sex, and even shopping addictions.[6] Internet and social media addictions, which affect up to 18 percent of adolescents, may have particularly damaging implications. One recent study observes that the teen depression and suicide rate both rose over 30 percent between 2010 and 2015 and are highly correlated with heavy levels of smartphone use. While there may be other key contributors, we are clearly in uncharted territory in terms of understanding the impacts of sustained technology use on human physiology.[7]

We are a disquieted culture full of disquieted souls. The cultural statistics are in plain sight. But in order to understand how disquiet really takes hold of us on a personal level, we need to understand its underlying pathology, or what I call the *Demons of Disquiet.*

The Demons of Disquiet

I've named the Demons of Disquiet *Threats, Over-Control,* and *Coping Mechanisms.* In my experience, these three elements operate together, laying the foundation for nearly every type of disquiet we experience.

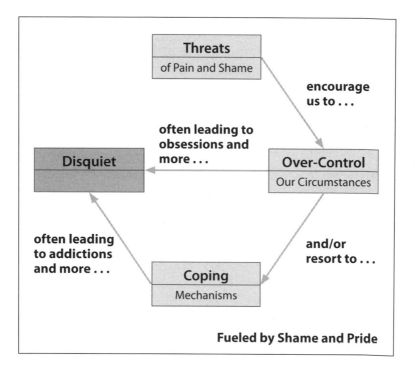

Threats are imagined or anticipated life events having the potential to cause us pain. Threats of pain can come in many forms—not only physical but emotional—such as shame-based feelings of rejection and devaluation, feelings of abandonment, and the loss of personal security. Because disquieted souls are fueled by various combinations of shame and pride, we are *hyper-sensitive to emotional pain* like ridicule, rejection, and humiliation.

While everyone naturally tries to control their circumstances, the disquieted soul is given to *Over-Control*. Because shame and pride are inherently self-protective, we go to extreme lengths to anticipate and manage any threat that might bring us pain. However, the worry, anxiety, and obsessive behavior stemming from this over-control increases our disquiet. The more distressed we feel, the more we try to over-control, often leading to a perpetual cycle of emotional turmoil.

None of us can control all of life's situations, and the combination of anxiety over threats, stress associated with over-control, and feelings of helplessness often drives us to use *Coping Mechanisms* to adapt or escape. These coping mechanisms can be substances like drugs or alcohol; process behaviors like sex, gambling, and gaming; or control behaviors like perfectionism. Whatever form we choose, we try to avoid anxiety or despair, often replacing it with something that offers us the illusion of escape or control. But, in the end, *the coping mechanism itself often becomes our functional master*. These *Cruel Masters* are the topic of the next chapter.

Everyday People . . . Like Us

The Demons of Disquiet can be difficult to understand conceptually, but they are easy to see in everyday tormented people—just like us. For example . . .

Susan is an adult who had a tough upbringing, with harsh and demanding parents. She is now living on her own but is still anxious about the pain their criticism can bring when they disagree with her life choices. She feels out of control and powerless to deal with her parents' criticism, so she resolves never to give them any reason to ever shame her. She resorts to obsessive people-pleasing techniques, but she lives with constant dissonance. Her soul is tormented, and she is a slave to her perfectionistic lifestyle.

John is a corporate executive who has had a successful sales career. But his company has a new CEO, and several of John's counterparts have recently been let go. His anxiety rises as he fears for his job, and he feels powerless to change the outcome. He busily prepares his résumé and refreshes his professional connections but can't shake the fear that his job may be coming to an end. Not coincidentally, John finds himself increasingly familiar with a given place at the bar, where he can calm his anxieties for a while. The "liquid courage" makes him feel more powerful, and with a drink in his hand, he can stand up to the world. But his soul is anxious and he is increasingly enslaved to the barroom.

Randy is a successful professional who grew up with a learning disability and was picked on as a child. He entered adulthood with a chip on his shoulder, worked harder than the rest, and achieved a position of prominence in his company. But he still hears the critical voices and imagines that people are laughing at him behind his back. He tries to control his life by keeping everything just right. He wants the perfect image, the perfect wife, the perfect children, and the perfect presence on social media. But under the surface, he is constantly dissatisfied. He is a disquieted slave to his perfectionism.

Karen is a high school senior. All her life she has lived up to her parents' expectations and done everything they asked. She is good at math and science, and her parents are pushing her hard to enter engineering school. But her passion is working with others, and she really wants to work in behavioral health. She knows her parents would be very unhappy with this choice because it doesn't pay as well, and she feels powerless to do what she really wants in life. Her grades begin to plummet, she is increasingly depressed, and her mind is filled with suicidal thoughts. Her soul is beleaguered and she is a slave to hopelessness.

Kelly and Jack have been married for five years, and his highly demanding personality is beginning to take its toll. Kelly is increasingly anxious about his strict expectations and strong criticisms of her but feels powerless to change him. She has always been fit, but she becomes increasingly obsessive about her body image. She grows more dissatisfied with the way she looks and consistently sees herself as overweight. She has begun taking laxatives and venturing into unhealthy fasting. Her soul is distressed and she is a slave to eating disorders.

Sharon is the mother of a talented, aspiring gymnast. She feels she must do everything to support her daughter, including bringing in more money for sports camps and the best club in the region. However, she is increasingly conscious of other talented team-members and wonders if her daughter is going to be able to break out of the pack. Sharon is afraid her daughter will fall short and begins cozying up to the coach to get preferential advantages. No matter what, however, she can't shake the envious comparisons with the other kids that keep running through her mind. Her soul is irritable and she is a vicarious slave to her child's success.

Pete is by nature an introvert, whose parents tended to neglect him in youth. He grew up on his own, proud of his self-sufficiency, but always hears painful voices of rejection in his head. He struggles with feelings of insecurity and abandonment, believing he has no control over them. Over time he has carved out a life where he can live withdrawn, isolated, and alone. His soul is harassed, and he is a slave to the self-protected isolation he has created to steel himself against others.

Every one of these scenarios illustrates the Demons of Disquiet in action—the threat of pain and powerlessness, attempts at over-control, often resulting in the use of and ultimate dependence on coping mechanisms.

If life were simple and we only dealt with one type of threat, we might be able to isolate and care for the problem like a doctor diagnoses and treats a stress fracture. But life is not so simple, and the path of a disquieted soul is not so linear. The Demons might be coming at us in many different ways at the same time. Worse yet, as our disquiet escalates, it can build on itself, like rungs on a ladder. Stress begets stress. Some psychologists have observed that we begin to feed on the constant rush of adrenaline and cortisol our bodies produce when confronted with stressful situations. We are harried, restless, and unstable, and we often can't break the coping cycle. We become, some experts say, addicted to stress itself, all the while *running away from our own unhappiness.*

> When [Jesus] saw the crowds, he had compassion on them, because they were harassed and helpless, like sheep without a shepherd. (Matthew 9:36)

Disquieted souls are the harassed and helpless of our modern age.

QUESTIONS FOR REFLECTION AND DISCUSSION

1. Reflect on the quote, "If we're dancing as fast as we can, then we don't have to think or get immersed in what's not being satisfied in our lives. . . . We're running away from our own unhappiness." How much of that describes you?

2. Do you often find yourself feeling threatened by physical pain—like illness—or emotional pain—like ridicule, rejection, and humiliation? How many of those threats actually come to pass? What techniques do you use to over-control or cope?

3. Review the short vignettes at the end of this chapter. Which one(s) sound most like you? Write one about yourself.

CHAPTER 3

CRUEL MASTERS

Sometime in 2013 I wrote myself the following letter. I titled it *Cruel Master*.

You should be angry every day at alcohol—for the life it has sapped away—for the family relationships it has shortened—for the opportunities it has wasted. But more days than not, you will treat it indifferently and ambivalently. You won't think much about it until it's time for a drink.

Each day, when it's time for a drink, consider that it's a habit that you don't have to follow—you've proven that before. But you treat it as a reward after a long day or a way to chill out and relax. More often than not, especially on the weekends, you're just bored.

After you've accommodated the habit another day, consider:

You're anesthetized for another day—a little more docile and a little less alive. A little more gray, dull, and complacent. A little more indifferent toward others and toward yourself.

You will eat more and exercise less. You will gain weight. You will be lazy. Your energy level will be low. You will not work out. You will look old and tired.

You will likely pass out on the bed at night. You may not even say goodnight to your family, let alone talk to them, read with them, and pray with them. You are gradually passing out on your entire life.

You will wake up in the middle of the night regretting the time you didn't spend with others. You may remember a Facebook post or e-mail you regret because you were drunk and angry or your judgment was impeded when you pushed "send."

You will wake up for another day with less energy. You will drag through the early part of the morning and revive in the afternoon—just in time to feed the bottle again.

You think no one notices, but they do.

It doesn't have to be this way. You've stopped before but you keep starting again because you keep forgetting the things that make you angry at the Cruel Master. You tell yourself this time it will be different. *You keep forgetting and you keep going back.*

When I resolved to address alcohol because of its oppressive hold on my life, I forced myself to read this letter every day and commit anew that I would not take a drink. Such a technique might work for some and not others. But every disquieted soul who has ever experienced the Demons of Disquiet knows that our coping mechanisms—alcohol in my case—ultimately become Cruel Masters.

I've redrawn the figure from chapter 2, showing these Cruel Masters as our coping mechanisms. More importantly, I show that *all Cruel Masters are ultimately an attempt to meet our deepest human needs*—or what I call our Identity-Needs.

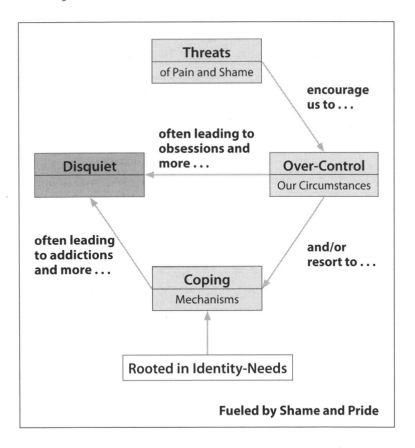

Kind Friends and Deepest Needs

All Cruel Masters begin as kind friends. They come to the door of our disquieted souls with a warm smile, comforting voice, and a thoughtful gift. They bring us a hot drink on a cold winter day. They speak reassuring words when we feel lonely and down. They bring comfort and gently calm our jittery hearts. They tell us that we matter—that we're special—*and everything is going to be all right.*

Cruel Masters know what we need most. They know our identity-needs, and they meet us in those special places. They know we need to *feel valued.* They know we need reassurance that we are not disposable—that we're not a piece of paper blowing away in a windstorm. They know we have a deep-rooted need to make a difference— to feel significant. They know we need to feel that we truly matter.

Cruel Masters know that we need to *feel secure*—that we hate feelings of vulnerability. They know how much better we feel when the winter storms come but food is in the pantry and the fire is warm. They know that we desperately need to feel safe and comforted. They know that, no matter how tough and rugged we may appear, we feel better with a warm blanket on our bed and a strong lock on our door.

Cruel Masters know that we need to *love and feel loved.* They know we long for days that we can hold someone, taste their lips, kiss their soul, and feel their heart. They know we yearn for a depth of love that brings feelings we've never felt before. And they know we need another to feel the same for us.

Cruel Masters know that we *hate pain*—and desperately want to avoid it. They know we hate physical pain, but we may hate pain in our souls even more. They know we hate the pain of loss—the waves of sadness, the sickness to our stomachs, and the endless holes in our hearts. They know we hate the pain of rejection, abandonment, and loneliness. They know we hate the pain of feeling overlooked, dismissed, and discarded. They know how much we hate to hurt.

Cruel Masters come knowing our deepest needs and offer a thoughtful gift to meet them. Cruel Masters come as thoughtful friends *but they leave as deceptive betrayers.*

Times, Ways, and Degrees

Cruel Masters all come to the door with one thing in common—they all offer to meet our identity-needs with something that makes us feel very good. In every case I cited in the previous chapter, the person had a deep need that was threatened by the storms of life. And the Cruel Masters came knocking.

Cruel Masters also have another thing in common. Most of them are not, in and of themselves, bad. In fact, they are usually very *good things*, like food, drink, talents, sex, beauty, family, professional success, or a lover. They are God's good gifts to us, intended to bring fulfillment, happiness, and pleasure to our lives.

But, as C. S. Lewis keenly observes in *The Screwtape Letters*, when God's good gifts are twisted, they quickly become life's Cruel Masters. As the demonic Uncle Screwtape tells his junior apprentice:

> Never forget that when we are dealing with any pleasure in its healthy and normal and satisfying form, we are, in a sense, on the Enemy's ground. I know we have won many a soul through pleasure. All the same, it is His invention, not ours. He made the pleasures: all our research so far has not enabled us to produce one. All we can do is to encourage the humans to take the pleasures which our Enemy has produced, *at times, or in ways, or in degrees, which He has forbidden*[1] (italics mine).

This is the Cruel Master's secret. It comes as a thoughtful friend with the best of intentions. But we choose to use its gift at the wrong time, in the wrong way, and in the wrong amounts—and it leaves us as a deceptive betrayer. It could not deliver what we hoped it would. It could not deliver what we needed.

Of course, we learn this too late—after the disquieted soul is an actual or a functional addict. As Screwtape continues, "An ever increasing craving for an ever diminishing pleasure is the formula."[2] In other words, we need *more and more* and it delivers *less and less.*

More and More for Less and Less

Many writers refer to Cruel Masters as idols, functional saviors, or counterfeit gods. Many observe that Cruel Masters are good things that we turn into ultimate things, and therefore they become our objects of functional worship. That is, they start out as something designed to serve us, and *we end up serving them.* Here lies the true power of the Cruel Master—we give ourselves to it, desperately hoping it will deliver us from our fears and anxieties in a world spinning out of our control. We want so badly for these things to deliver us. To make us feel like we will matter—forever. To make us feel safe and secure—forever. To hold our face and kiss our souls—forever. To make the pain go away—forever.

But they don't. They can't. We keep coming back over and over again. We need more and more of them—and they deliver less and less.

Screwtape's "ever increasing craving for ever diminishing pleasure" is easy enough to see in substance addiction. One drink turns into two, which turns into five. A couple of cigarettes a day turns into one pack, which turns into two. Fentanyl begins to manage pain and ends by managing an entire life. The strong physiological effects associated with these substances are plain. We need more and more of the substances, and they deliver less and less.

This is also increasingly easy to see in process addictions like eating, compulsive gambling, gaming, and sex. Scientists tell us that the pleasure centers of our brains "light up" when exposed to enjoyable events. We become addicted to the pleasure associated with the process and keep coming back for more. But scientists also tell us that these pleasure centers can be overstimulated, overexerted, and numbed. Hence, we need more and more and they deliver less and less.

This is even apparent with social media addictions. In 2017 Facebook's founding president Sean Parker remarked that the firm's founders consciously relied on the addictive power of dopamine, associated with receiving post *likes*. This was, in his words, the way Facebook could "consume as much of your time and attention as possible."[3] But many are burning out on social media platforms because they, too, demand more and more and deliver less and less.

Money-making can have the same psychological effect as process addictions. In addition to its economic value, research indicates that money appeals to increased psychological feelings of achievement, respect, and freedom.[4] However, above a certain annual income level—$75,000 to $120,000 in America today—money appears to have a point of diminishing returns.[5] Beyond that, money ceases to be a way to meet our needs and becomes an unending, if not vain, pursuit. Studies show that more money does not lead to more satisfaction in fact, many of us become less charitable, less concerned with others, more entitled, and more self-absorbed.[6] But we chase it anyway. It demands more and more of our time, our energy, and our focus. And it too delivers less and less.

What About Love?

As we've seen, much of the Cruel Masters' power can be explained through observing physiological and psychological impacts. We are, after all, pleasure-seeking people, and we can quickly form behavioral habits and addictions centered on receiving that pleasure. However, in my experience more that physiology and psychology is at work. The Cruel Masters' power also involves a deep spiritual element. And the best example of that spiritual element is seen through the power of love.

Religion and psychology seem to agree on at least one thing—our most basic primal emotions are fear and love. Love, of course, is the emotion we write thousands of poems and songs about. The lyricists tell us that love is the answer, love is all we need, love is everything, and love is a battlefield.

Whatever the lyrics, there can be little doubt about the power of love. Science now informs us that a number of powerful neurochemicals are at work in its forming, particularly during the early stages of romantic love. Of all of them, oxytocin seems to get the most attention. But, while some have attempted to characterize love as a purely chemical process, I don't think most of us believe that. And those who do probably don't succeed too well in relationships. I think most people believe their most intimate relationships may include, but run much deeper than, mere biology.

For many disquieted souls, it is love, more than anything—even career and money—that we throw ourselves at. The human objects of our love can be the greatest sources of our desires. But any such object of our love can quickly become the cruelest of masters, because we come to them with our *deepest needs* and our *deepest demands*. We look to them to give our lives meaning when we often don't find it in ourselves. We look for their admiration, adoration, and validation. We want them to fill up the holes in our damaged souls. We are enraptured by their attention. We bathe in feelings of security when they are next to us. We love to feel their touch and hear their voice nearby. It takes away our shakiness. It sooths all those fears.

The disquieted soul idealizes the objects of its affection. The lover becomes more beautiful than life itself. Poetry and music is full of lovers as our angels and our dreams come true. The disquieted soul is only okay when it is validated by its deified object of love. We need look no further than the mother who can't let her son go. We needn't go far to find the needy lover who can't exist in this world without their partner. We know the obsession of fatal attraction.

Disquieted souls are a wellspring of never-ending needs for validation, security, love, and pleasure. As Pastor Tim Keller observes:

> The self-glorification that we need in our innermost being, we now look to get from our love partner. The lover becomes the way to fulfill one's very life. *The worth and meaning that you desperately want comes from the loved one*[7] (italics mine).

And our loved ones—even the best intentioned of them—simply cannot deliver. We give our idealized, deified objects of love more and more of ourselves, but we get less and less in return. In his book, *The Denial of Death*, Ernest Becker reflects on the futility of seeking our life's value from a love interest. As Becker writes:

> We get back a reflection from our loved objects that is less than the grandeur and perfection that we need to nourish ourselves. We feel diminished by their human shortcomings. Our interiors feel empty or anguished, our lives valueless, when we see the inevitable pettinesses of the world expressed through the human beings in it.[8]

In other words, as Keller states, "no created thing can bear the freight of our deepest hopes or the weight of our soul's longings."[9] Ironically, our lovers can become the greatest Cruel Masters.

Our Own Undoing

By now, we have hopefully realized that the Cruel Master is really not the lover—nor food, drink, talents, sex, beauty, family, success, or money. Used the right way, these are God's good gifts to us, intended to bring pleasure, meaning, and fulfillment to our lives. They become our addictions and our functional gods only because *we ask them to.*

The cruelty of it all is when, to use Becker's words, we look to these things for "the grandeur and perfection that we need to nourish ourselves." We bring our empty, deformed, and powerless souls and look to these things to deliver us—*to fix us.* We use them in times and ways and degrees they were never created for. That is the cruelty of it all. The disquieted soul creates its own Cruel Masters. It plants the seeds of its own undoing.

In the end, what the Bible says is plain to see. "They exchanged the truth of God for a lie, and worshiped and served created things rather than the Creator—who is forever praised" (Romans 1:25).

QUESTIONS FOR REFLECTION AND DISCUSSION

1. Review the section on Kind Friends and Deepest Needs. What are your deepest needs? What are the Cruel Masters you tend to use to meet them?

2. Have you ever thrown all your needs for validation, security, love, and pleasure at another person, like a romantic partner? What is or was the outcome?

3. Do you consider yourself enslaved to any Cruel Masters? If so, after reading this chapter can you diagnose the reason for this slavery?

CHAPTER 4

THE DRIVEN

" Because it's there."

Those words, often attributed to Edmund Hillary but actually spoken by George Mallory, have come to personify the voice of The Driven. Like Hillary, who conquered Mt. Everest in 1953, Mallory was driven to achieve the same feat some 30 years earlier. Unlike Hillary, Mallory died falling short—less than 300 meters from the summit. Conrad Anker, who discovered Mallory's mummified body in 1999, described his state:

> The pose in which Mallory had come to rest said a lot about his final moments. His head was uphill, and his arms were in a grasping-type position, probably trying to arrest a descent that was out of control. Then there was the snapped rope around his waist and a broken leg. It seemed that he had died struggling.[1]

Such are The Driven. They achieve or they die struggling. They achieve, achieve, and achieve some more, and they still die—*struggling*.

Our world would likely be unrecognizable without The Driven. They are the explorers who circumnavigated the entire world in wooden ships. They are the journeyers who achieved manned space travel with computers less capable than our smartphones. They are the pioneers and captains of industry who tamed America's vast frontiers. They advance the fields of science and medicine. They create majestic musical compositions, novels, and works of art. They extend the limits of sports performance. They build start-ups into trillion-dollar businesses.

The Driven achieve at every level. A select few are household names and the subjects of biographies. Many more perform equally amazing feats at less recognized levels. They are the artists, the creators, the athletes, and the academically inspired. They are the inspirations whose accomplishments we marvel at regularly—striving to conquer their corner of the universe.

While The Driven do not come packaged in a single personality type, a few common descriptors reoccur. Type A personalities, for example, take the shape of hyper-competitiveness, impatience, and perfectionism. They can also tend toward hostility and emotional distance, focusing on wealth, status, or power.[2] While many see Type A behavior as a little unhealthy, The Driven are rewarded and encouraged by it. The Driven live in a world of "constructive dissatisfaction"—or just plain dissatisfaction—and we encourage them to do so. As Marcus Buckingham writes:

> A leader's job is to rally people toward a better future. Leaders can't help but change the present, *because the present isn't good enough.* They succeed only when they find a way to make people excited by and confident in what comes next[3] (italics mine).

He is right. Leadership is about future-casting and always moving forward, and The Driven are all about moving forward. The Driven are compelled by, even consumed with, the next thing. Their common denominator is that whatever has been done—whatever they have done—must always be improved.

The Dark Side of Achievement

But our greatest strengths are often our greatest weaknesses. The greatest weakness of The Driven is that we often can't shut off our drive—or our frail egos. Whether we are driven by pride's demand for self-importance or shame's cry to prove our self-worth, our achievement obsessions can take hold in every corner of our lives. And these obsessions often come with unintended consequences. Modern leadership gurus regularly opine about this. For example, Marshall Goldsmith provides a running catalog of bad personal behaviors he has regularly observed through coaching successful leaders. His list of habits like making destructive comments, telling the world how smart we are, withholding information, not listening, failing to express gratitude, blame-shifting, and claiming undeserved credit, reflects just a handful of these ugly characteristics.[4] And that ugliness tends to spill over beyond the boardroom into personal relationships across all areas of life.

To be fair, not every leader possesses every one of Goldsmith's traits or even most of them. But plenty exist to go around. And our culture is prone to give The Driven a pass. They are, after all, so successful. When our cultural heroes put their vanity or ugliness on public display, we rationalize it by speaking of their genius or reflecting on their many past accomplishments. We deify them, reckoning that mere mortals could not understand the pressures of their undertaking.

Those of us who identify among The Driven tend to give ourselves a pass as well. We often subscribe to what Goldsmith refers to as "the success delusion." Because we have tasted success—at whatever level—and are so driven to succeed, we often assign all success to ourselves and any failures to others. He writes:

> This wacky delusional belief in our godlike omniscience instills us with confidence, however unearned it may be. It erases doubt. It blinds us to

the risks and challenges in our work. If we had a complete grip on reality, seeing every situation for what it is, we wouldn't get out of bed in the morning. After all, the most realistic people in our society are chronically depressed.

But our delusions become a serious liability when we need to change. We sit there with the same godlike feelings, and when someone tries to make us change our ways we regard them with unadulterated bafflement.[5]

In other words, what might be great for success in all our earthly pursuits can be deadly when it comes to truly examining ourselves and realizing the need to change. For all our giftedness, The Driven may be the most prone to disquietude. Dangerously, we repress and ignore the disquiet, *or we see it as a friend.* More restlessness leads to more achievement. More dissatisfaction leads to more conquest. We hear words like peace, joy, and contentment, and they sound fluffy and weak—like stuff for the old folks' home. They are alien concepts. They might be okay for others, but they are certainly not for us—at least not now.

Ultimately, we believe this at our own peril. A few self-aware hyper-achievers learn this sooner rather than later. Reflecting on unhappy early career choices designed to achieve his personal significance, one author writes:

I've learned my demons aren't just mine. Thousands of young people share the same thirst to achieve that I had (and still have)—rising out of family pressures, alienation, and an identity that they're smart or talented or special or destined to do something significant. On the plus side, it can make them hard-charging, industrious, and willing to put themselves out there. On the flip side, it can be paralyzing. It can lead to depression, a sense of isolation, even self-destruction. I think it's harder in an era of social media, where there's always something you're missing.[6]

Indeed, we disquieted hyper-achievers are missing something. But it isn't to be found through notching yet another achievement. It is found when we actually come to our senses and are honest about what our drive is doing to us.

That Would Never Happen Here

It would be convenient to say the dark side of achievement is limited to The Driven living outside the body of Christ. However, experience tells us this is far from the case. The church provides fertile soil for its own Driven to strive, achieve, find mass adulation, and realize their dark side. Each week provides a visible forum for pastoral achievers to put their skills on display before a captive audience. Of course this is not the intent, but it is an easy enough trap to fall into—particularly in the age of YouTube and social media.

Like any organization, churches provide the opportunities for fan fcedback that achievers desperately require. Over twenty years ago, Pastor Alistair Begg commented:

> Why do you think it is that so many prominent and useful pastors have ended up in the slag heap over the last five years? I'll tell you one of the reasons. Because they were not honored in the way that honor is genuinely due, namely the prayerful accountable encouragement of the people of God. But they were adulated and they were idolized and they were fawned over and they were made much of and they began to believe that junk — and they toppled from their flimsy little pedestals.[7]

Two decades later, hundreds more prominent and useful pastors have toppled from their pedestals. The proverbial rock-star achiever who rises to fame through charisma, transformational leadership, and powerful oratory falls into some moral failing—usually (and not coincidentally) sexual. Speaking today on the topic of pastoral addictions, one expert notes:

> Seminaries are full of addicts in training, because seminaries are full of idealistic perfectionists. Perfectionism leads to compulsive behaviors, and they don't present themselves as problems initially *because you get rewarded for them*[8] (italics mine).

Of course pastors are an easy group to assess because their achievements and failings are on full display. But the church has plenty of hyper-achieving congregates to go along with them. We are the believers who have realized success in our fields or some ministry, gained status and recognition within the church, and demonstrated more of Goldsmith's observed behaviors. We add our two cents to every discussion, pass judgment, speak when angry, negatively explain why that won't work, make excuses, cling to the past, play favorites, fail to express regret[9]—and so on.

In short, The Driven all tend to swim together in the same pool, whether inside or outside the church. While those of us in the church might expect to see significant personal differences due to the sanctifying work of Christ, we often do not. We tend to behave the same as all the other Driven, because we learn to be content with our "respectable sins" and our disquieted souls. In American Christianity, the deep and often painful changes that tear out the roots of shame and pride remain rare indeed.

At least they have been for me.

Because It Was Forbidden

As I proposed in the first chapter, the engines fueling this behavior lead back to shame and pride. While shame drives some to live in the shadows, it drives others to prove ourselves to the world at any cost. Since we only hear voices of criticism, we rise up to prove the doubters wrong. Ironically, many of The Driven who begin in shame often reach to pride to get us where we want to go.

In other words, Jekyll's Shame summons Hyde's Pride.

Pride emboldens us to believe enough about ourselves that we dare to reach for the impossible. That part of it shows up when The Driven think big, strive, and achieve. Then the destructive part kicks in. And despite our modern tendency to paint over it with euphemisms like self-confidence and "reaching for our dreams," it's not hard to see when pride has gone too far. As Os Guinness writes:

> The classical and Christian view is that the sin of pride is wrong and deadly because it is inordinate and overweening. As the Oxford English Dictionary defines it, pride is "an unreasonable conceit of superiority," an "overweening opinion of one's own qualities." Consider its synonyms: egotism, arrogance, hubris, selfishness, vanity, haughtiness, presumption, boastfulness, bigheadedness, self-satisfaction, self-centeredness, and the like. None of them is admirable.[10]

I have never met a high achiever without an overweening self-opinion. Some keep it in check, balancing it with a reasonable level of humility. But others let our runaway pride take us all the way down the path of destruction—to the land of St. Augustine's pears.

In his famous confession of the stolen pears, Augustine writes of desiring to do evil simply for the sake of evil itself.

> Late one night—having prolonged our games in the streets until then, as our bad habit was—a group of young scoundrels, and I among them, went to shake and rob this tree. We carried off a huge load of pears, not to eat ourselves, but to dump out to the hogs, after barely tasting some of them ourselves. Doing this pleased us all the more because it was forbidden. Such was my heart, O God, such was my heart—which thou didst pity even in that bottomless pit. Behold, now let my heart confess to thee what it was seeking there, when I was being gratuitously wanton, having no inducement to evil but the evil itself. It was foul, and I loved it. I loved my own undoing. I loved my error—not that for which I erred but the error itself. A depraved soul, falling away from security in thee to destruction in itself, seeking nothing from the shameful deed but shame itself.[11]

Of course some rather gifted people don't see the big deal in all of this. "Rum thing," wrote Justice Oliver Wendell Holmes to Harold Laski in 1921, "to see a man making a mountain out of robbing a pear tree in his teens."[12] But this is to severely miss the point. Augustine's lesson has nothing to do with pears. Rather, it has to do with Augustine's recognition that, deep inside his being, he wanted to do evil simply because it was evil. As he writes, "Doing this pleased us all the more because it was forbidden."

In my experience, the worst manifestation of pride is to actively sin just for the thrill of sinning. And we can get to that point; our estimation of self becomes so high that we find ultimate satisfaction in tempting fate or testing God, as the case may be. We get a high from living dangerously and being smart or talented enough to get away with it. We live on the edge because it makes us feel alive to outsmart all the things that might catch us.

Stealing the pears can be a metaphor for any area of life where we cross the line for the thrill and excitement of crossing the line. It's fun. It makes us feel superior—*especially if we naturally feel inferior*. Because deep down inside, we want to pretend the rules don't apply to us. We are, after all, so successful. This is when the darkest side of The Driven takes root—when we convince ourselves that we're really above it all. This is the disquieted soul at its worst—when it begins to love the process of its own undoing.

"'You will not certainly die,' the serpent said to the woman." (Genesis 3:4)

But she did.

QUESTIONS FOR REFLECTION AND DISCUSSION

1. Do you consider yourself among The Driven? Do you know what forces tend to drive you? Do you consider it a healthy or unhealthy driven-ness?

2. Review the section titled "The Dark Side of Achievement." Do any of these behavioral tendencies describe you?

3. Review the section titled "Because It Was Forbidden." Have you ever found yourself doing something wrong just for the thrill of doing something wrong? If so, do you know why?

CHAPTER 5

DESPAIR

From my youth I have suffered and been close to death;
I have borne your terrors and am in despair.
Your wrath has swept over me;
your terrors have destroyed me.
All day long they surround me like a flood;
they have completely engulfed me.
You have taken from me friend and neighbor—
darkness is my closest friend. (PSALM 88:15-18)

This is the conclusion of Psalm 88. It is unique in that, while many psalms speak to despair, they conclude by lifting their eyes up in praise. Psalm 42, for example, asks, "Why are you downcast, oh my soul?" and concludes by reminding itself to put its hope and praise in "my Savior and my God."

Not so with Psalm 88. It seems to be planted in God's field of poetry as a reminder that sometimes we live in a world of sadness, where we feel pounded and defeated by the overwhelming waves of life—and we can't lift our eyes up. We simply don't have the strength.

All of us have felt this type of deep sadness to varying degrees. Some of us are among The Driven left exhausted and defeated. Some of us have battled Cruel Masters and find ourselves deeply wounded. Some of us have felt deep loss and cannot escape the anguish of our soul. A heavy blanket of sorrow drapes over our shoulders. The waves pound relentlessly. Whatever the circumstances, our disquiet stems not from anxiety but deep sorrow. We are forlorn. Darkness is our closest friend.

We want to sleep—and sometimes we want to put ourselves to sleep forever.

Depression

I enter this topic with great caution, recognizing that different people struggle with these feelings in varying degrees. Some of us have journeyed through months or even years of this darkness, propelled by personal loss, rejection, or betrayal. The wounds are deep and the sadness severe, but the reason for the grief is discernable. Others, however, struggle for no evident reason at all. And those who struggle with clinical depression are not just struggling with a spiritual issue. As one source writes:

> In 2013, Lifeway Research conducted a survey which revealed that 48 percent of Evangelical Christians believed that "prayer and Bible study alone can overcome serious mental illness." While

it is important for Christians to see a spiritual dimension to managing or experiencing some degree of healing in their mental health, the study may point to a failure to realize that mental illness is a real illness, an illness involving the body.[1]

The piece continues, "People can suffer from cancer, a broken leg, or the flu and, like depression, these are physical realities."[2] As the noted preacher Charles Spurgeon, whom some believe suffered from bi-polar disorder, wrote, "The troubled man experiences a good deal, not because he is a Christian, but because he is a man, a sickly man, a man inclined to melancholy."[3]

Like Spurgeon, Martin Luther's *anfechtung was highlighted by bouts of severe depression. As one author observes:*

Luther's depression was always marked by the same features: a feeling of profound aloneness, a sense that God was singling him out for suffering, a loss of faith that God is good and good to me, and a resulting inward self-reliance. Luther's depression only intensified under the burden of the Reformation's unforeseen fruit. The more that regularly hurting Christians sought him as a physician of souls, the more acutely he felt the weight of responsibility for his teaching and writing. He couldn't shake the notion that the reforms he advocated might destroy—rather than revive—the church. Sickness, unbelief, and anxiety conspired and drove him to the brink of despair.[4]

As some have noted, if they were living today, both Luther and Spurgeon might be medically treated for their conditions. Yet, as with anyone, it is difficult to know how much of their depression was purely biological, versus habitual and environmental. Both of them felt the heavy burden of responsibilities that often drove them to extreme mental exertion. Both of them encountered periods of loneliness, particularly Luther, during his exile to Wartburg Castle. Spurgeon seemed particularly impacted by changes in the weather.

There lies the rub with major depression, as well as anxiety. It is unclear where biology starts and ends. As the Harvard Medical School writes:

> It's often said that depression results from a chemical imbalance, but that figure of speech doesn't capture how complex the disease is. Research suggests that depression doesn't spring from simply having too much or too little of certain brain chemicals. Rather, there are many possible causes of depression, including faulty mood regulation by the brain, genetic vulnerability, stressful life events, medications, and medical problems.[5]

This is where the medical analogy of the broken leg fails. Generally, a broken leg can be clearly observed, diagnosed, and treated. The cause of depression is much more complex and its treatment much more variable. Clinical depression is not an exemption from the malady of a disquieted soul—in fact it may be both a cause and effect. The turbulence and instability of the soul's disquiet may indeed act as a catalyst for depression's genetic predisposition. Depression, in turn, weighs heavily on the soul's disquiet. One feeds the other, which feeds the other—and so it goes.

The obvious answer, therefore, is to treat both body and soul together. In the case of the body, this may require medication, and this bears no shame. It may also require better eating, sleeping, and living habits. In the case of the soul, it may require some deep introspection into the roots of our disquiet. This is not to blame the victim. It is to acknowledge that no one is exempted from a disquieted soul because no one is exempted from sin and its effects.

Self-Pity

However, a version of despair exists that should be treated more squarely, and that is the version driven by self-pity. As I previously stated, a disquieted soul is often a despondent soul—withdrawing in self-pity when it doesn't get its way. And none of us—not even the godliest—are exempt.

Few studies in contrast are greater than those of Elijah the prophet in 1 Kings 18 and 19. By any fair reading, we appear to be witnessing the lives of two different men. In the earlier chapter, Elijah presents himself before all Israel, along with the 450 prophets of Baal and 400 prophets of Asherah who "eat at Jezebel's table." His challenge is simple—to see whether Baal or the Lord God of Israel could miraculously consume an offering with fire. After one of the most powerful throwdowns in the biblical narrative, the Lord displays his power by raining fire from heaven upon the altar, Elijah puts the prophets of Baal to death, and he caps it off by running at superhuman speed past the chariot of Ahab.

Then the story takes a bizarre twist. Upon learning of Elijah's destruction of the prophets, Queen Jezebel sends a message essentially stating, "You're a dead man." Elijah responds by running like a coward for his life, sitting under a tree, and asking God to kill him.

Elijah's boomerang into fear and despondency is sudden, but it lingers for a long while. Even after being revived and continuing the journey for over a month, Elijah's despair remains. When he is finally given a chance to speak with God on the matter, he exclaims:

> I have been very jealous for the LORD, the God of hosts.
> For the people of Israel have forsaken your covenant,
> thrown down your altars, and killed your prophets

with the sword, and I, even I only, am left, and they seek my life, to take it away. (1 Kings 19:10 ESV)

Such is the mark of a disquieted soul living in self-pity. It sees only itself in the circumstances and resents circumstances that don't go the way it desires. It begins to marinate in its own performance, read its own press releases, and deeply begrudge anything that resists its self-importance. In short, as Alistair Begg comments, Elijah had done great things, but it appears his own self-estimation had overtaken him.[6]

Elijah is not alone. Around 100 years earlier, the prophet Jonah went to extreme lengths to avoid God's command to preach repentance to his enemies in Nineveh. After conceding and fulfilling his mission, Jonah made a shelter to the east of the city, where he waited to watch Nineveh burn. But it didn't. In his compassion, God spared the repentant Ninevites—and Jonah fumed. Seeing God's relent as "very wrong," he sulked and complained. He complained because he failed to get what he really wanted—to see his enemies perish.

Like Elijah, Jonah only saw himself in the circumstances and deeply resented their failure to go the way he desired. Like Elijah, Jonah went into a tailspin, threw himself into self-pity, and asked to die. In his final statement of despondency, he cried out, "I am so angry I wish I were dead." Unlike Elijah, the Bible does not record Jonah's recovery from this despondency. The narrative runs out on Jonah's disquieted soul.

Such scenes aren't limited to Jewish prophets. According to history, Haman was second in command in the Persian Empire during the reign of Xerxes I. As recorded in the book of Esther, Haman had the ear of the king—so much so that he successfully secured a decree for the destruction of all the Jews living in Persia. Haman was living large. But he possessed a fatal flaw, exposed by Mordecai the Jew.

Although a fairly obscure man, Mordecai made a habit of not bowing or genuflecting to Haman—and that insult infuriated the noble. In one particularly galling moment, while returning home from Esther's party, Haman saw the defiant Mordecai at the king's gate and it threw him into a free fall. According to the biblical record:

> Calling together his friends and Zeresh, his wife, Haman boasted to them about his vast wealth, his many sons, and all the ways the king had honored him and how he had elevated him above the other nobles and officials. "And that's not all," Haman added. "I'm the only person Queen Esther invited to accompany the king to the banquet she gave. And she has invited me along with the king tomorrow. But all this gives me no satisfaction as long as I see that Jew Mordecai sitting at the king's gate." (Esther 5:10–13)

I return to what I wrote of Elijah and apply it verbatim to Haman. Such is the mark of a disquieted soul living in self-pity. It sees only itself in the circumstances and resents their failure to go the way it desires. It begins to marinate in its own performance, read its own press releases, and deeply resent anything that resists its self-importance. In short, Haman's self-estimation had overtaken him. So much so that he had to go home and tell his friends all about himself.

In all these examples, flawed self-estimation presents the underlying problem. We have come full circle to the deepest issue of our soul's disquiet. Even in despair, the issues again are shame and pride.

A Difficult Message

It's difficult to tell someone living in despondent self-pity that the underlying problem is a flawed sense of self. After all, we are hurting. We are nursing wounds. We are in deep pain. How dare anyone tell us that we are the problem?

This is doubly difficult when genuine despair exists from genuine loss. For example, I can only imagine the heavy blanket of anguish and sorrow associated with burying a child. Similarly, I can't personally identify with the deep pain of living with years of chronic medical conditions. Or the trauma of broken families ravaged by mental illness.

Yet, I've observed that among some of us, even our pain can become a badge of honor. Or it reinforces the shame we naturally feel. "No one else has felt what I've felt." "No one else can understand my suffering." "Nobody knows what I am going through." *Me . . . only me.*

This problem becomes particularly evident when we begin determining what others should and should not say to us on the topic. We begin posting rules or critiques in blog posts. Or we make sure everyone on social media happens to remember our pain through vaguebooking—and we are offended when they do not. Or we engage in perpetual attention seeking, continually managing our attitude, appearance, and conversations to remind others of our pain.

Such is the insidious wickedness of the human heart (Jeremiah 17:9). Shame wallows in its own pity, viewing itself as too inferior to receive comfort. Pride parades its pain in front of the world, seeking anything by which it can prove its self-importance. In the end, the common denominator is *self.* Even in despair, shame and pride perpetually fuel the churning instability of disquiet.

The Blessing of Despair

The silver lining in all of this is that honest despair, more than anything else, can drive us to realize our deepest moments of need. It can be a hidden blessing to be among The Driven left exhausted and defeated. It may be God's kindness to let us battle with Cruel Masters and find ourselves deeply wounded. Some of us need to feel deep loss and the anguish of our soul. Some of us need to be constructively undone.

Deep crisis, more than anything, can drive two responses. On one hand, we can become bitter, jaded, and resigned to the worthlessness of life. We can continue to live in the shadows, sulking in our circumstances and swimming in self-pity. We can dance with suicidal thoughts and even carry them out—if by no other means than a slow descent into isolation.

Or we can step up and be honest about our soul's disquiet. We can begin to see the underlying spiritual maladies that govern our lives. We can reach out to God, asking him to lead us through an honest personal inventory.

We can begin to resolve the Human Paradox.

QUESTIONS FOR REFLECTION AND DISCUSSION

1. Do you regularly struggle with bouts of depression and despair? If so, what steps are you taking to address this?

2. Do you find yourself withdrawing in self-pity when you don't get your way? If so, write down a few situations when this occurred. What caused it and what was the outcome?

3. Are you experiencing deep crisis in your life? If so, are you living in the shadows of avoidance and denial? Would you be willing to reach out to God and ask him to help you honestly address the reasons for your soul's disquiet?

CHAPTER 6

THE HUMAN PARADOX

In 1946 Jean Paul Sartre delivered a defense of his atheistic existentialism titled *Existentialism Is a Humanism*. He states if God does not exist, then human existence necessarily precedes human essence. In Sartre's words, "Man first of all exists, encounters himself, surges up in the world—and defines himself afterwards." In short, our sense of self develops out of nothing into whatever we will it to be. Sartre concludes that a person is defined only by what he makes of himself.[1]

Although I am clearly not an atheist, I think Sartre is onto something important. As we become self-aware, we immediately try to make sense of our existence. A person's sense of self begins with an acute sense of nothingness, and he constantly strives to create some meaningful self-concept. Therefore, to use Sartre's terms, we are always trying to "make something of ourselves." Any modern marketing campaign makes this plain.

Sartre's error is in failing to recognize that God *does* exist and, deep within us, we also have an embedded sense of God's existence. As the apostle Paul writes to the Roman church, God's presence is written on the hearts of men (Romans 1:20 and 2:15). We may try to shake it, as Sartre appears to, but it lingers, like Lady Macbeth's "damned spot." Because of this, mankind, despite our sense of nothingness, is simultaneously conscious of the existence of something "infinite in being and perfection." And we instinctively know that we are tethered to it.

I propose that this explains what I call the Human Paradox.

- We need to feel meaningful, but we feel meaningless.
- We need to feel worthwhile, but we feel worthless.
- We need to feel safe, but we feel insecure.
- We need to feel powerful, but we feel powerless.
- We need to feel valued, but we feel disposable.
- We need to feel esteemed, but we feel ashamed.
- We need to feel loved, but we feel unlovable.

We feel empty—and our disquieted souls rabidly seek to control our circumstances to enable us to meet these identity-needs. But we are too deformed to do so alone.

Not "Born Okay the First Time"

Part of the reason I do not believe the Bible is just another fairy tale written by unsophisticated primitives is that, within the first three chapters, it goes directly to the central issue of human existence and identity. Like Sartre, every advanced philosopher gets there—*but the Bible starts there.* Humanity's sense of self has always been central to any thoughtful discussion; humanity's enemy goes after it, right out of the gate.

> "You will not surely die," the serpent said to the woman. "For God knows that when you eat of it your eyes will be opened, and you will be like God, knowing good and evil." (Genesis 3:4–5)

In other words, "You can really do a lot better than the identity God gave you—he is holding out on you." And the rest is history. The fall of man, as Christianity describes it, is the biblical reason we begin with Sartre's sense of nothingness. Or, as I prefer to call it, *emptiness.*

There's a tag line that's been around for a few decades reading, "Born okay the first time." This is a somewhat snarky modern response to the term "born again"—an attempt to convince ourselves that we've come into this world just fine, and we don't need to be fixed. But, deep inside, I think most of us know that isn't true. If it were, the Human Paradox wouldn't be so obvious and problematic. We would come out of the womb having all our identity-needs met—or at least having a clear means to meet them. We wouldn't feel so empty and dissonant. *But we do.*

Returning to my earlier words, our soul's disquiet ultimately stems from a haunting desire to recover paradise lost. We have a sense of our spiritual Creator, "infinite, eternal, and unchangeable, in his being, wisdom, power, holiness, justice, goodness, and truth."[2] And that Creator's fingerprints are written into the fabric of our being. We desperately feel the identity- needs that he designed into our souls. We need to be meaningful, worthwhile, secure, powerful, valued, esteemed, and loved. Those are the attributes we were designed to partake in. And we instinctively grasp for them, like a baby grasps for its parent's finger.

Only one problem exists—the fall has left us deeply deformed. When we come into this world, our spiritual essence is like a broken mirror. The remaining reflection is sufficient to show us what we were designed for, but we are cracked in hundreds of places. Spiritually, we enter life like a withered tree—twisted, gnarled, and lifeless. It is easy enough to see the beauty and form we were intended for, but that beauty has been replaced by ugly deformity.

We understand physical human deformity. Although we have compassion for those born with birth defects, we immediately notice them. While spiritual birth defects aren't obvious in the delivery room, if we are honest with ourselves, we don't have to live too many years before we understand that something is very wrong. This is the essence of the Human Paradox.

We enter this world with powerful identity-needs—but meeting them is beyond our grasp.

Our grasping is futile. But it doesn't keep us from trying.

Futility

We have arrived at the ultimate root of the disquieted soul. Disquiet is born out of shame and pride, but shame and pride have their origins in our *flawed sense of self*. Shame stems from recognizing our deep defects and trying to cover them up. Pride stems from sensing the splendor of our Creator and seeking that splendor for ourselves. That is why I previously stated that, paradoxically, the disquieted soul constantly *tries* to feel superior while *actually* feeling inferior.

So I return to where I began. At the beginning of this book, I wrote:

> The disquieted soul is constantly worried and dissatisfied. It is impatient, overdriven, and reckless. It moves from one thing to the next—seeking and pursuing that one thing or person it believes will bring complete happiness. It worries about unforeseen threats and obsessively tries to control imagined circumstances. It hungrily seeks to overachieve, while often feeling devalued and unappreciated. It feels needless levels of misunderstanding and rejection and immerses itself in self-pity.
>
> The disquieted soul takes careless and reckless risks to feel alive. It lives in a world of disillusioned extremes, seeking invented ideals this life cannot offer. It is often talented and successful by the

standards of this world, but it is incapable of enjoying its own success. The disquieted soul is tormented in its unrest and lives in a constant state of disappointment.

And now we understand why. The disquieted soul desperately struggles to meet its deepest identity-needs— the needs with which it was designed. And, as I wrote, in its deformed state,

[The disquieted soul] engages in a perpetual battle to manage all its circumstances in the belief that it alone knows what is truly best. It cannot stand uncertainty because it trusts no one and nothing more than itself. The disquieted soul presumes godlike omniscience, demanding that life conform to its plans. And when life does not, it worries and rants, pouts and anesthetizes.

Yet despite its natural position at the center of the universe, the disquieted soul constantly battles against the reality that the universe is too big for it to handle. Like a child trying to seat itself on a throne, the disquieted soul vainly tries to occupy the place of God, all the while flailing in its human limitations.

Thus, we come to the end of it all—the futility of living life separated from our Creator. It is the futility of "chasing after the wind." It is the "Vanity! Vanity!" proclaimed by the teacher in Ecclesiastes. It is our soul's disquiet as we toil under the sun, live among The Driven, love our Cruel Masters, maybe fall into despair—and then go away. Another generation comes and goes—and another—and another. The sun endlessly rises and sets. The winds keep blowing and the streams keep flowing. *It's all futile.*

It's all futile because, whether our names are captured in the pages of history books or we have buildings and institutions named after us, we never solve the Human Paradox within ourselves. No matter how much we achieve or how much others may talk about our legacy, we live an entire lifetime with that desperate sense of emptiness. We don't talk about it—in fact we often mock it. We keep ourselves busy so we don't have to think about it. We find hobbies or love interests to occupy our hearts for a season. Then they leave. But the Human Paradox remains. We try and try—but we can't solve it. Because the answer lies outside of ourselves.

I have come that they may have life, and have it to the full. (John 10:10)

Here begins the deliverance of the disquieted soul.

QUESTIONS FOR REFLECTION AND DISCUSSION

1. Read each of the identity-needs associated with the Human Paradox. Which one(s) (meaning, worth, safety, power, value, esteem, love) most resonate with you?

2. Read appendix A and reflect on shame and pride. Why do you think I say both shame and pride come from a flawed sense of self?

3. Does your life feel futile? Do you still feel empty after trying everything to meet your identity-needs? Are you willing to honestly seek God's hand of deliverance in a new and fresh way?

PART II
DELIVERANCE

CHAPTER 7

DEEP IN OUR BONES

I f Jesus is the answer, what is the question? Variations of this phrase have been circulating for some time, and different people have provided different answers. For those struggling with disquiet, I'll try to do the same.

Most of you reading this book probably belong to the Christian faith. Like me, you may have claimed Christianity for years, if not decades. You have listened to hundreds if not thousands of lectures and sermons. You may have even delivered them. You've read dozens if not hundreds of books. You may have even written them. But perhaps you're still reading this book because, deep down inside, you haven't been able to deal with your soul's disquiet. Perhaps you've come to a point, as I did, where you seriously doubt whether you really believe what you profess. You've walked the aisle. You've sung the songs. You've listened to the sermons. You've written the checks. You may have even dedicated your life to Christian ministry. But your soul is not quiet. It is not healthy. You know something is very wrong.

Others reading this may not claim the Christian faith. You may have read this far because something resonated with you. You may be living with the Demons of Disquiet, constantly cycling through various threat, control, and coping issues. You may have come to see Cruel Masters for who they truly are and found yourself in their bondage. You may be among The Driven, finding yourself on the achievement treadmill and feeling increasingly disillusioned. You may be in the depths of sadness and feel that darkness is your closest friend. You may truly know the anguish of a disquieted soul and see no way out. You may have experienced the Human Paradox in all its frustrations and found life increasingly futile.

Whether or not you consider yourself a Christian, the questions are really the same. Does Jesus, who is called the Christ, actually provide a path of deliverance for our disquieted souls? And if so, *how*?

Skin-Deep

I assume that most readers are familiar with the basic tenets of the Christian gospel. For those who are not, I provide a short synopsis as appendix B to this book. I also offer you this parable:

> I once was a young orphan living in the streets of poverty, not unlike the poorest areas of India or Africa. I regularly dug through the garbage pile for

food. My clothes were torn, I rarely bathed, and I stank. I lived among a band of other orphans in the slums, knowing no other life but that of being "naked, wretched, and blind."

One day a king ventured from a mountain land far away. He was dressed so splendidly that when he stood before me I could scarcely look at him, and I didn't want to. He was beautiful; I was ugly. I hated him in my heart. But his eyes caught mine and captivated me.

He extended his hand, and he said, "Lane, you are my son, and today I have become your father." He put my head close to his heart, he cleaned me, he took his clothes and put them on me, and he began to lead me to his home—our home—far away in those mountains. As we journeyed together, he began to teach me the ways of being a child of the king—how to speak, how to think, how to treat others, how to think of myself. It was very different for me, not at all like my time in the slums, and many times I messed it up. But whenever I stumbled along that journey, he helped me back up, put my head against his heart, corrected my steps, and set me back on that course toward the mountain. And we're still journeying together.[1]

This is a parable of spiritual restoration—of being chosen, redeemed, cleansed, and adopted into the family of the king. It is a parable of being given a new life and a new destiny. It is also a parable of learning to actually *live* as a member of that new family.

These are the themes of the Christian message of salvation. We speak of being bought back and delivered from our captivity to sin. We speak of being declared righteous and having all our sins forgiven through the atonement of Jesus Christ. We speak of being adopted into the family of God, with God as our new Father and Christ as our elder brother. We speak of receiving a new identity in Christ, because of our new place in this royal family. We speak of receiving new life through the power of Christ's resurrection. We speak of living holy lives because our Father is holy. Sometimes teachers use more formal theological terms like redemption, justification, substitution, adoption, and sanctification—but the concepts are the same.

All of these truths are remarkable and life-changing. Many people have fallen to the ground in wonder and thanksgiving over having such grace extended to them. Many people who have felt like that orphan in the slums are overwhelmed by the privilege of becoming children of the king. It's a story that, when baked into our souls, we should never get over.

Therein lies the rub. All of these truths can be understood, and even experienced to a degree, without getting baked into our souls. They don't necessarily get *deep in our bones.* Christians have understood this problem for a long time. We use slogans like the need for God's truth to get from our head to our heart to our hands. Like the smell of a new car, once the experience of salvation begins to fade, life often becomes business as usual. We know the language and terms. But we haven't really changed very much. We have a faith that is skin-deep.

While addressing the issue of deep change, Tim Keller tells the story of a college acquaintance who became a Christian. Previously, the man had slept around—in fact, he admitted to using sexual conquest as a means to get his identity-needs met. Keller relates that once this man became a Christian, he cleaned up his act and stopped sleeping around. However, not coincidentally, he tended to be very domineering in Bible studies. His identity-need (Keller calls it a need for power) still wasn't being met by God. It just transferred from sexual conquest to the need to be right in class.[2]

In my experience, this story is representative of a vast number of Christians—including myself. We can experience a faith that is skin-deep. It may even get below the dermis. (Being domineering in class, for example, is more acceptable than sexual promiscuity in most Christian circles.) But it does not get deep in our bones. Our souls can be as disquieted as anyone else's. And they often are.

Clearly, in order for a disquieted soul to be delivered, this needs to change. The question is, how?

Turning the Corner

Not long before I began writing this book, I was force to conduct a serious spiritual inventory. My life had gone a direction that required me to take a hard look in the mirror and address some uncomfortable realities about myself. At one point in the process, I remember saying, "I don't even know who I am anymore."

I'm guessing many of us have said that at some point in life. When we say it, we're usually not dealing with physical amnesia. We still remember our names, professions, life histories, and so on. We aren't questioning the facts about who we are. We are questioning the essence of our identity— our very *sense of self.*

Over the last decade, many books and talks have dealt with the believer's identity in Christ. They delve deeply into many of the themes I summarized earlier—our redemption, justification, adoption, servanthood, and so forth. These books stand alone and don't need repeating. Instead, I will center on the most important element of identity that is most critical for setting the soul on a path to deliverance.

Let's return to shame and pride.

No Self-Condemnation

Therefore, there is now no condemnation for those
who are in Christ Jesus. (Romans 8:1)

This well-known passage of Scripture introduces what
teachers call justification—the fact that Jesus paid the
penalty for our lifetime of sins against God. We are no longer
guilty criminals in God's court of law; Christ's sacrifice on
our behalf has set us free.

This spectacular truth should command our attention
each day. But an equally spectacular truth speaks to those
of us held in bondage to shame.

There is no longer any *self-condemnation* for those who
are in Christ Jesus.

Shame lives in the world of self-condemnation. It hears
any and every voice of disapproval—its own being the
loudest. Shame always feels inferior, constantly failing to
live up to its own standards. Shame always feels unworthy.
When we live in a world of shame, we often find ourselves
running to sin because that's what we were destined for
anyway. We are bad people. *Shame always makes us feel like* √
bad people.

Those of us in bondage to shame hate being humiliated,
mocked, and ridiculed because those things remind us of
what we already believe about ourselves. And this is where
we need to take the message of Christ. It wasn't coincidental
that Jesus's crucifixion was a criminal's death by the most

humiliating means. The vivid accounts of his being stripped naked, mocked, slapped, spit on, and ridiculed aren't just part of an interesting story. The Scripture says Jesus "endured the cross, scorning its shame" (Hebrews 12:2). He *overcame shame* exactly the same way he overcame sin.

Jesus put shame to death. And when we are "in Christ," Jesus puts our shame to death as well.

The term "in Christ" is critical. It is the basis of what teachers call our union with Christ. As John Stott stated:

> The commonest description in the Scriptures of a follower of Jesus is that he or she is a person "in Christ." The expressions "in Christ," "in the Lord," and "in him" occur 164 times in the letters of Paul alone, and are indispensable to an understanding of the New Testament. To be "in Christ" does not mean to be inside Christ, as tools are in a box or our clothes in a closet, *but to be organically united to Christ, as a limb is in the body or a branch is in the tree.* It is this personal relationship with Christ that is the distinctive mark of his authentic followers.[3] (italics mine)

To be in Christ means we are so connected to him that everything he has done, we have done through association. Everything he has accomplished, we have accomplished. Everything he has overcome, we have overcome. Everything he has put to death, we have put to death.

Jesus put shame to death. And if we are in Christ, we no longer need to live in shame's identity because it isn't ours anymore. The voices inside need no longer mock us, ridicule us, and insult us. They need no longer scream, "Disapproved." Even when people tell us those things, we need no longer own them. Those voices have been put to death. The only voice that ultimately matters anymore is God's voice—the voice that belongs to us because we are in Christ.

And God's voice to us says, "Lift your head up. Lift your eyes up. Come out of the shadows. You don't need to hide anymore. You don't need to hate yourself anymore. You're not a bad person. I know you by name—and I approve of you."

No Self-Congratulation

If there is no longer any self-condemnation for those who are in Christ Jesus, there is *no longer any self-congratulation either.*

This should almost go without saying. If we have come to the end of ourselves, recognizing our inability to solve the Human Paradox and our absolute need for God's gracious redemption, it would seem odd for pride to still live in our home.

But it does. Pride lives in the world of self-comparison, always seeking self-congratulation. It seeks any and every voice of applause—its own being the loudest. Pride always seeks to feel superior, believing that it needs to stand above everyone else. To cite C. S. Lewis, pride always wants to be the "big noise at the party" and is constantly annoyed if anyone else is acting like the "big noise." Pride gets no pleasure out of having something, only out of having more of it than the next person.[4] Pride always makes us feel like we are above the rest.

Those of us in bondage to pride hate seeing awards, recognition, status, and acclaim going to anyone but us. Our self-comparison defines us. This is the key to recovering our identity from pride. We must learn the same lesson we learned with shame: Our voice is no longer the one we should be listening to.

The apostle Paul gives us this truth in 1 Corinthians 4. When his status as an apostle is being unfairly attacked, he responds that his accusers' opinions don't really matter. He then goes a step further and says, even *my own* opinion of myself doesn't really matter. The only opinion that matters is God's.

When he came to earth as a man to live in our stead, Jesus also put pride to death. If we are in Christ, we no longer need to live in the identity of self-comparison because that identity isn't ours anymore. The voices inside need no longer seek to congratulate us, inflate us, and exaggerate us. They need no longer scream, "Compare yourself! Be sure you're better! When others want to make themselves the "big noise," we need no longer pay attention to them. The only voice that matters anymore is God's voice—the voice that belongs to us because we are in Christ.

And God's voice to us says, "I created you as one of a kind. Since the beginning of time there has never been another person like you. You don't need to compare yourself to anyone else. You are and always will be of inestimable value. You no longer need to congratulate and honor yourself. I know you by name—and I honor you."

The identity message for the disquieted soul—whether driven by shame or pride—is the same. We need to stop listening to our own voice—and we need to start listening to God's.

My sheep listen to my voice; I know them, and they follow me. (John 10:27)

QUESTIONS FOR REFLECTION AND DISCUSSION

1. Spend time reflecting on the forces that shape your sense of self. Perform an honest personal inventory and then write down your true opinion of yourself. Who are you and why are you that way? Write the answers as if only you and God will ever see them.

2. Reflect again on appendix A. What voices have you trained yourself to hear? Do you tend to hear shame's voices of self-condemnation? Do you tend to hear pride's voices of self-comparison followed by self-congratulation?

3. What techniques have you trained yourself to use to deal with your personal shame? Can you identify with the shame-pride cycle? If so, how does it operate in your life?

4. How can being "in Christ" change your sense of personal identity? How is it that "in Christ" self-condemnation and self-congratulation no longer apply?

5. Why is it important that we stop listening to our own voice and start listening to God's?

CHAPTER 8

THE PATH OF
IDENTITY

Will the real Lane Cohee please stand up?

If I were ever to play *To Tell the Truth*, this would mark the point in the show where I would stand and two imposters would remain sitting. No matter how convincing they had been throughout the show, we would finally get to the truth of the identity question. Of course, discovering that truth is the fun of it.

In conversations about identity, we often spend time considering our name and what we know about it. We typically think about our family name and its origins. Among some cultures, including ancient Israel, names are often intended to reflect a given personal characteristic. Hence, when the names of people like Abram, Jacob, Simon (Peter), or Saul of Tarsus were changed, we recognize that those people were being re-identified at their very core. Similarly, our adoption into the family of God re-identifies us. It's not just a name change. We actually take on a new personal identity through our union with Christ.

Knowing who we are resonates with us at a very deep level. Writers and movie-makers have used many plots to dance with this identity theme. However, as transformational as this may be, I don't believe it is the right starting place for the disquieted soul. For those of us bred out of shame or pride, I am convinced that we need to shift our thinking. The ultimate question is not *Who am I?* but *Who knows who I am?*

Or as the old saying goes, it's not who you know—it's who knows you.

I Know You by Name

In the previous chapter I used a phrase to encourage those harassed by the voices of both shame and pride: "I know you by name." But the phrase is not mine, it is God's.

The story of Israel's exodus from Egypt is a familiar one. After God provides a way for Israel to escape their Egyptian bondage, the Israelites (not coincidently) fall into another form of bondage—to idolatry. In Exodus 33 God appears to be ready to abandon them, but Moses intercedes on their behalf. In verse 11, the text states that, "The LORD would speak to Moses face to face, as one speaks to a friend." So Moses appeals to that relationship. He reminds God that the Israelites are his people and asks him not to give up on them. At that point God relents, stating to Moses, "I will do the very thing you have asked, because *I am pleased with you and I know you by name*" (verse 17, italics mine).

The phrase "I know you by name" is not the same as "I know your name." Lots of people know our names, but few know us deeply and intimately at the very core of our being. God is effectively saying to Moses, I am the King of the universe. I know you deeply and intimately, at the core of your being. *And I am pleased with you.*

When I was a young Air Force lieutenant, I had the opportunity to work a special assignment for my commanding general officer. The general was known for being demanding and difficult to please, so I approached the assignment with some trepidation. But after we finished, he said, "Lane, I was never worried about it—because I knew you were."

That statement sticks with me 30 years later because it was a statement of approval from an important person whom I admired. Yet, ironically, I saw the man years later after his retirement, and he didn't remember me. I wasn't surprised, but it speaks to the depths of our identity message. We can get so much value out of an event like that—from a human who ultimately doesn't even remember us. What if we really believed that the King of the universe knows us to the core of our being *forever*—and approves of us *forever*?

We might be tempted to think God only has this type of deep, intimate relationship with special people like Moses.

That's not the case. In John 10, Jesus makes reference to each of his followers when he states:

> Truly, truly, I say to you, he who does not enter the sheepfold by the door but climbs in by another way, that man is a thief and a robber. But he who enters by the door is the shepherd of the sheep. To him the gatekeeper opens; the sheep hear his voice, *and he calls his own sheep by name* and leads them out. When he has brought out all his own, he goes before them, and the sheep follow him, for they know his voice. (John 10:1–4 RSV, italics mine)

In a world of 7.5 billion people, when you belong to Christ, the King of the universe knows you uniquely by name. He knows you to the core of your being. He knows every distinct feature and every rare quality. He knows every strength—and he knows every weakness. He created you for a unique purpose and he delights in you. He approves of you.

In the end, that's what matters most. We naturally begin with the question, "Who am I?" Instead, I propose we begin with the questions, "Who knows who I am?" and "Who does he say that I am?" Because it's not about who we know—it's about who knows us.

Paradigm Shift

Thomas Kuhn's *Structure of Scientific Revolutions* represents one of the most influential writings of the last century, if for no other reason than that it turned "paradigm shift" into a household phrase. This term is often invoked to describe a significant change in perspective. But that isn't the whole story.

According to Kuhn, normal scientific discovery follows a pattern of slow, incremental development until, at some point, a crisis of perspective occurs. Enough new facts develop that our standard set of assumptions can no longer contain them. At that point a period of scientific crisis, turmoil, and dislocation occurs, until a new way of thinking or set of assumptions is developed. Hence the radical and transformational shift in paradigms emerges.[1]

If it hasn't become clear by now, I am suggesting the disquiet and dissonance in our souls should be driving us to consider a radical and transformational shift in our *identity paradigm*. No matter how many years we have claimed Christ, we have likely bought into an existing set of identity assumptions that keeps us stuck in our behavior patterns. We constantly live out the Demons of Disquiet and remain the harassed and helpless because we have not changed our basic thought patterns about ourselves. We continue to look *inside* ourselves. We have not shifted our perspective.

In order to do that, let me offer three basic changes of thought:

- Change the voice you hear.
- Change your identity source.
- Change how you meet your identity-needs.

I addressed the first change in the previous chapter. We are naturally preconditioned to listen to our own voices. This will always cause us problems—particularly if we are bred in shame and pride. Shame will falsely condemn us. Pride will compare us—and then try to falsely congratulate us. Either way we are constantly listening to the wrong voices. They are the voices that keep us swimming in a spiritual cesspool. We need to train ourselves to stop listening to our own voice and start listening to God's voice. We need to stop the "self-talk," whether positive or negative, because when we listen to ourselves, we lead ourselves astray. I can't overemphasize this. This message is exactly the opposite of what any self-help teacher will tell us. But it is the only true beginning to deliverance. This demands a radical change in thinking.

Earlier in this chapter I addressed the second change. When we consider our identity, we naturally start with *I*. We think of our names, our background, our talents, our career, and so on. Again, the focus is us and what we think about ourselves. While the Bible has a lot of important things to say about us, I will again suggest that we should first think about the one who knows us by name. We should reframe the natural question, "Who am I?" Instead we should ask, "Who does God say that I am?" What God says about our identity is immeasurably more important than what we say about our identity. This is what we need to capture. This demands a radical change in thinking.

To address the third change, let me return to the list of identity-needs I previously offered.

- We need to feel meaningful.
- We need to feel worthwhile.
- We need to feel safe.
- We need to feel powerful.
- We need to feel valued.
- We need to feel esteemed.
- We need to feel loved.

In chapter 6 I observed that the Human Paradox besets us because, for the disquieted soul, every one of those identity-needs remains ultimately unmet. We get a little of this and a little of that. We fall in and out of love. We welcome a new job until it gets old. We get recognized for an achievement and then it is forgotten. We make some money, then we need more. On and on it goes.

Worse yet, we turn to Cruel Masters to meet our identity-needs. As I've written, these Cruel Masters come as thoughtful friends with the best of intentions. But we choose to use them at the wrong time, in the wrong way, and in the wrong amounts. They leave us as deceptive betrayers. In many cases, they leave us actual or functional addicts. They don't deliver on their promise; they leave us undone.

The resolution to the Human Paradox is, of course, to have our identity-needs fulfilled in Christ. Imperfect as it is this side of eternity, this relationship is always the best solution to our identity-needs. We ultimately need God to affirm us. We ultimately need God to honor us. We ultimately need God to give us security. We ultimately need God to give us true love. No better source exists. Yet, while this is true, it is still a pat answer. It doesn't get deep in our bones—until we start down the path of the first two changes. This demands a radical change in thinking.

To see this radical change, we need to go to a spiritual boot camp. We need spiritual circuit training to *change our ruminations*.

QUESTIONS FOR REFLECTION AND DISCUSSION

1. Why do I say that the ultimate identity question is not *who I am* but *who knows who I am*? Do you agree?

2. Reflect on God's phrase, "I know you by name." How might you think about yourself differently if you really believed God knew you by name, knew everything about you, and delighted in you? Why is this fact *actually* true for the Christian?

3. Return to your most important identity-needs and how you tend to meet them. Have you ever committed to truly finding your identity-needs in Christ? If you have and it hasn't really stuck, why not?

CHAPTER 9

RUMINATIONS

We take captive every thought to make it obedient to Christ. (2 CORINTHIANS 10:5)

Six months before my eldest son was married, I challenged myself to don a suit for the wedding that I hadn't fit in for fifteen years. It wasn't going to be easy because, since then, I had gained over forty pounds. But research tells us that event-based goals are the best way to motivate human change. So I put myself on a diet and fitness routine and successfully lost the weight. Only time will tell if I keep it off.

The common denominator with all training regimens— be they physical, academic, or spiritual—is *discipline*. Change is hard work, and the longer we have practiced bad habits, the harder it is to change. But in God's strength, change is possible. In order to reform the identity of the disquieted soul, we need to begin with our ruminations.

Discipline

Each of us instinctively knows how to discipline our thoughts. For example, as college students taking a high-pressure test, we likely told ourselves to calm down and think clearly. In a competitive environment, we direct ourselves to get our heads in the game. We understand self-direction. We know how to coach ourselves when we need to.

The problem with self-coaching is that it is hard work. It requires active focus and discipline. It's much easier to passively let our minds drift wherever they naturally take us. And the souls of disquiet naturally drift to all the wrong places. Many of our identity meditations are based in things like worry, shame, or pride. We get hold of a line of thinking like a dog gets hold of a bone. We chew on it and chew on it some more. In fact the Hebrew word for meditate *(hâgâh)* actually suggests *mental chewing*. And the bone we're usually chewing on isn't a good one.

Breaking the meditations of disquiet takes discipline. The discipline of meditation, which I detail in appendix C is learned, not naturally occurring. However, it involves a process that we encounter in almost every area of life—often without even knowing it. Engineering and management textbooks are filled with it. It's called *active feedback control,* and it consists of three simple steps that need to happen over and over again, every day.

Stop and Think, What am I dwelling on?
Ask whose voice am I listening to?
Adjust to God's truth.   *Repetition*

Active feedback control is not complicated, but it requires recurrence. Recurrence is discipline that requires us to re-train our thinking patterns in ways that do not happen automatically. I would no sooner *just* change my thinking than I would have *just* lost 40 pounds. It's hardest in the beginning. But it can be learned.

For example, Susan is ruminating on her demanding parents again and getting increasingly anxious. In the middle of an imaginary conversation about her parents' disapproval, she stops herself. She thinks, "What am I dwelling on?" Then she asks herself, "Whose voice am I listening to?" She knows the critical voices emerge from her deep sense of shame. She adjusts, praying that God would give her truth about herself and the situation.

John is imagining another downsizing action at work and worrying about the hammer falling on him. He anticipates his co-workers ridiculing him as he packs up his things and walks out the door. At that point he stops himself. He thinks, "What am I dwelling on?" He asks himself, "Whose voice am I listening to?" He knows his fear of losing his position comes from his own deep sense of pride. He adjusts, praying that God would give him truth about himself and the situation.

Randy is imagining people laughing at him behind his back again because they think he is stupid. He begins to congratulate himself on his accomplishments and achievements. He counters with the thought of posting more vanity shots on social media. At that point he stops himself. He thinks, "What am I dwelling on?" He asks himself, "Whose voice am I listening to?" He knows that the imaginary voices come from his own deep sense of shame. He adjusts, praying that God would give him truth about himself and the situation.

Karen is feeling overwhelmed again about the prospect of her parents' disapproval. She begins to host more dark thoughts about her life. At that point she stops herself. She thinks, "What am I dwelling on?" She asks herself, "Whose voice am I listening to?" She knows her fear of disapproval comes from her own sense of shame. She adjusts, praying that God would give her truth about herself and the situation.

Kelly is dwelling on Jack's humiliating comments. She imagines him coming home and criticizing her again. Her thoughts go back to fixing her body. At that point she stops herself. She thinks, "What am I dwelling on?" She asks herself, "Whose voice am I listening to?" She knows the pain of humiliation comes from her own deep sense of shame. She adjusts, praying that God would give her truth about herself and the situation.

Sharon's daughter had a mediocre gymnastics per-formance, and Sharon is growing more anxious. She hears the laughing voices of the other mothers as they parade their girls around the gym. She begins to think about ways she can further promote her daughter. At that point she stops herself. She thinks, "What am I dwelling on?" She asks herself, "Whose voice am I listening to?" She knows her need to compare her daughter comes from her own deep sense of pride. She adjusts, praying that God would give her truth about herself and the situation.

Pete is replaying his parents' rejection and having more imaginary conversations with them in his head. He thinks about how he doesn't need them anyway. At that point, he stops himself. He thinks, "What am I dwelling on?" He asks himself, "Whose voice am I listening to?" He knows his feelings of insecurity and abandonment come from his own deep sense of shame. He adjusts, praying that God would give him truth about himself and the situation.

In each case, active feedback control can begin to break the cycle of the Demons of Disquiet. But active feedback control is not a magic mantra. Neither is it something we can do one time and be done. There are no magic words. There is no magic prayer. We may need to pray over and over again for God to give us the truth about ourselves and the situation. And while I am definitely encouraging us to be in the moment, active feedback control is not some kind of mindfulness meditation. It is driving us upward, not inward.

Adjusting to the Truth

In the case of each person I previously described, I ended
the example with the phrase, "She adjusts, praying that God
would give her truth about herself and the situation." We
must understand that both things are in play. The truth
about *us* and the truth about *our circumstances* are two
separate and equally important things.

The truth about us comes back to our identity-needs.
As I've said, we need to change our thinking from what we
say about ourselves to what God says about us. If you are in
Christ,

- You have meaning because God made you a new
  creation.
- You have worth because God paid everything to
  redeem you.
- You are safe because God is your strong tower.
- You are powerful because God is the strength of
  your heart.
- You are valued because God delights and rejoices
  over you.
- You are highly esteemed because God created
  you for a unique purpose.
- You are loved because God finds you altogether
  beautiful.[b]

---

b   Derived from 2 Corinthians 5:17; Romans 8:31–32; Proverbs 18:10;
     Psalm 73:26; Zephaniah 3:17; Ephesians 2:10; Song of Songs 4:7.

For many years I could not accept these things about myself. I paraded around as a teacher of good theology, focusing on man's sinful depravity. That was actually shame masquerading as truth. While the Bible has a lot to say about people who are not in Christ and about our persistent struggles with sin, those are *not* identity messages for the believer. Every day we need to be reminded that we are saved by grace. And every day we need to be reminded that our identity is secure. Our identity-needs can actually be met, not by Cruel Masters but by God, our Good Master, when we get these truths deep in our bones.

Getting them deep in our bones—or deep in our hearts, as the case may be—requires active concentration and discipline. When we are feeling good about ourselves, we need to return to these truths and remember God's all-encompassing grace. When we are feeling bad about ourselves, we need to return to these truths and remember what God says about us. Whatever we are ruminating on, we need to constantly *Stop and Think, Ask,* and *Adjust.*

But as much as we need to adjust to the truth about us, we also need to adjust to the truth about our circumstances. Our identities never change, but our circumstances do. Active feedback control doesn't guarantee a certain outcome. Susan's parents may continue to be demanding. John might get laid off. Some people might actually think Randy is stupid. Karen's parents may fail to understand her perspective. Jack may continue to be critical. Sharon's daughter may never become a gymnastics superstar. Pete's parents really did reject him.

Our identities never change. Our circumstances do. But God is always at work, weaving his tapestry—even when we don't naturally see him.

That's why we also need to ruminate on The God of Our Circumstances.

QUESTIONS FOR REFLECTION AND DISCUSSION

1. Read appendix C and reflect on the practice of Christian meditation. Consider how this practice might change your natural daily thought patterns. Why is changing these thought patterns (ruminations) so important?

2. Return to the vignette you wrote about yourself in chapter 2. How might that vignette change if you trained yourself to consistently Stop and Think, Ask, and Adjust?

3. Review the section titled Adjusting to the Truth. Reflect on the identity statements. Will you commit to actively and consistently meditating on these truths so they get "deep in your bones?"

CHAPTER 10

THE GOD OF OUR CIRCUMSTANCES

I t hurts . . . make it stop!
Anyone who has had children or remembers childhood is familiar with such words. We hate to hear them from our loved ones. We hate to hear them from ourselves. Because *we hate pain.*

I suspect our biggest cultural problem with God involves the existence of pain and suffering—particularly our own. We live in a culture with a highly internal locus of control, which means that we believe we can control away much of our pain. This tees up the Demons of Disquiet because the threat of pain, more than anything, is the catalyst for our over-control and coping mechanisms.

For decades I have operated within a Christian tradition having a very high view of God's divine sovereignty, providence, and goodness. I have embraced many verses like Romans 8:28: "And we know that in all things God works for the good of those who love him, who have been called according to his purpose." But over time I have come to learn that my belief was only skin-deep. My intellect accepted God's providence and goodness, but my disquieted soul did not. The reason was simple. While I believed God was in control and might even have my good in mind, I was worried he would *still* let me hurt. And I didn't want to hurt.

If we are going to deal with our disquieted souls, we need to do more than correct our identity problem. We need to reframe *our view of God himself* in the midst of life's circumstances—particularly the painful ones.

Reframing Reality

Psalm 73 is a narrative about a reframed reality. It tells the story of a follower of God who becomes disillusioned about the way his world is operating. Everything is upside-down. The wicked prosper. They suffer no pain. They are strong and well fed. Even though they are corrupt and arrogant, they are rich—and getting richer. They are proud and they mock God, but they don't pay the penalty. In fact, the opposite is true—they only prosper more.

When the psalmist sees this, his confidence in God is deeply shaken. He begins to envy the wicked. Living for God seems all for naught. He begins to doubt everything he believes. Good things happen to bad people. Only the good die young.

Then the psalmist enters the sanctuary of the Lord. He sees the big picture. He perceives the ultimate destiny of the wicked. His perspective changes. He grieves the fact that he almost lost his faith. And he concludes with some famous words of Scripture: "Whom have I in heaven but you? And earth has nothing I desire besides you. My flesh and my heart may fail, but God is the strength of my heart and my portion forever" (Psalm 73:25–26).

His reality gets reframed.

In social sciences framing refers to the way our minds organize and interpret the data we absorb on a daily basis. In short, it's the way we make sense of reality, particularly when it comes to decision making. In the psalmist's case, his mental frame was dominated by the human circumstances around him and their seeming unfairness. He didn't see The God of Our Circumstances. He didn't see the bigger picture.

It's an easy mistake to make—one that happens to us all the time, particularly as modern people. Whether we are formally trained as scientists or not, our cultural training teaches us to view things from an entirely physical perspective. Believing an invisible God is divinely ordering everything into one eternal tapestry doesn't fit our view of reality. Our eyes aren't trained to see that way. Our minds aren't trained to think that way. Moreover, we are constantly distracted by all the cares of this world. And since he is invisible, how would we expect to see him operating, anyway?

Of course, the Bible has a lot to say about spiritual eyesight. In Ephesians 1:18 the apostle Paul's prayer for believers is that the "eyes of [our] hearts" would be opened. He is effectively praying for us to experience what the psalmist did. He is praying that we may look for The God of Our Circumstances in the midst of it all. He is pleading that we may see God intimately weaving every thread of his tapestry, using every person and circumstance of life around us. He is praying for us to use different lenses. In addition to our physical eyes, he's asking us to put on the spiritual equivalent of night vision goggles.

Again, this does not come naturally. It is no more natural for us to look for The God of Our Circumstances than it is for us to *just* lose forty pounds. We are back to the spiritual boot camp. We are back to getting truth deep in our bones. We are back to *Stop and Think, Ask,* and *Adjust*—regularly asking God to adjust our view of life's circumstances. Just like the psalmist had to.

Reframing reality is a spiritual discipline that never ends.

He Knows What He's Doing

Of course the biggest problem with our circumstances is that we don't know how they will turn out—until they do. We know how every finished story, including those from the Bible, turned out. We know Joseph went from the jail cell to royalty. We know Job was finally healed and was given a new family. We know Moses got to see the promised land but no more. We know Jesus was crucified but left the grave.

But what if we were the people living in the middle of each of those stories? What if we didn't know how they were going to end?

Of course, we hear the occasional refrain about how, in the end, God wins. While that's true, it doesn't tell me whether I am going to lose my job, die of this cancer, make enough money to retire, divorce my spouse, or ever feel like what I do makes a difference.

There's an old saying: "I may not know what the future holds, but I know who holds the future." That's all well and good, provided the one who knows the future has my comfort and happiness in mind.

This is a huge problem for the disquieted soul. The disquieted soul sees the potential for painful outcomes and instinctively starts taking matters into its own hands. As I previously wrote:

[The disquieted soul] engages in a perpetual battle to manage all its circumstances, in the belief that it alone knows what is truly best. It cannot stand uncertainty because it trusts no one or nothing more than itself. The disquieted soul presumes God-like omniscience because it demands that life conform to its plans. And when life does not, it worries and rants, pouts and anesthetizes. In short, the disquieted soul is never satisfied nor calmed, because it always has to be in control.

Of course, getting a better sense of our identity can help with this problem, but it does not entirely solve it. Because in the end, this problem also comes down to God's identity. Specifically, *does God know what he's doing* and *does he have my best interest in mind*?

Most of the time we can probably accept that "Father knows best." We know that if God is really all-knowing and "infinite, eternal, and unchangeable, in his being, wisdom, power, holiness, justice, goodness, and truth," he probably has matters under control—and they will probably ultimately work out well. We can read plenty of accounts of God's divine providence, where he entered the minutest details of life to work everything *just so*.

For example, we can read the book of Esther, where God's hand is so inconspicuous his name isn't even mentioned but a series of chance circumstances leads to the deliverance of the entire Jewish nation—so that the line of Christ might be preserved. We learn things that *just happen*—from a drunken king making an inappropriate request of his queen, to that queen being deposed, to the king picking just the right historical chronicle to cure his insomnia. We read how an unknown Jewish girl just happens to become queen and how her intervention is essential for Jewish deliverance. Her obscure uncle just happens to uncover a plot against the king and rise to prominence in the nick of time. We discover how some shrewd legal maneuvering just happens to reveal a means of saving the Jews, even after an irrevocable edict of destruction has already been signed. And if we understand its significance in the context of God's eternally redemptive plan, we understand why that young Jewish girl and her uncle who lived 2,500 years ago preserved the spiritual lineage of every twenty-first-century Christian today.

Scripture is full of similar examples where things *just happen*. Those are often the "oh, ye of little faith" moments, when we shake our heads at people who responded to uncertainty just like we do—because we know the end of the story and they didn't. We can probably reflect on situations in our own lives when we were panicked, until circumstances just happened to work out—often better than we could have hoped. We might even have looked at those circumstances in the rearview mirror and said, "I'm glad God was in control and I wasn't."

We can consider analogies from our own experience, when we were the parent or the expert and knew what we were doing. Maybe our kids or colleagues questioned our judgment and we responded with something like, "Don't worry—I've got this." We understand the parent-child illustrations in Scripture. We who have been parents remember times when we could see the big picture much better than our kids could. They were unsure. They were scared. They were afraid of the potential pain that lay ahead. We had to reassure them—sometimes over and over again—"Don't worry, I know what I'm doing."

Most of the time, these situations from Scripture and life make sense. But when the Demons come, we can easily lose perspective. And in those moments, we can imagine God our Father relating to us as scared children. We can see him getting down on a knee to look us in the eyes and say, "Don't worry. I know it's scary, but I know what I'm doing.

Then we might hear him say, "Remember the last time?"

Remembering to Remember

Remembering the last time is what God had in mind when he commanded the nation of Israel to lay the stones in Joshua 4. When Israel crossed into the Land of Promise, it was a major event—four decades in the making. The stones, not unlike our own national memorials, served as visual reminders of God's command to *never forget*. He said:

> When your children ask in time to come, "What do those stones mean to you?" then you shall tell them that the waters of the Jordan were cut off before the ark of the covenant of the LORD. When it passed over the Jordan, the waters of the Jordan were cut off. So these stones shall be to the people of Israel a memorial forever. (Joshua 4:6–7 ESV)

Of course, Israel quickly forgot. Not many generations later, they were back serving their Cruel Masters. That's why the discipline of remembrance is so essential—and so hard. On the roller coaster of life's circumstances, remembering God's faithfulness is the hardest thing to do. When we start slowly climbing up the tracks, we immediately forget the last ride. Life is scary. That's why we have to keep coming back to remembrance. We must remember from Scripture. We must remember from experience. We must remember from history. We must remember from analogy. When we are in the thick of uncertainty and we don't know how the story is going to end, we have to *keep coming back to remembrance.*

Remembrance is another spiritual discipline of intentional meditation and rumination. It's the reason we should write down our experiences and stories. And the reason I am writing this book—because we tend to forget.

Regular Meditations

Coaching ourselves to *Stop and Think, Ask, Adjust, Reframe,* and *Remember* requires ongoing discipline. Retraining our thought patterns demands continuous reminding and recurrence. One of the best ways to reinforce this training is through the practice of regular Christian meditation. I have provide a detailed explanation of this practice in appendix C.

In my experience, meditation regularly cleanses the palate of our souls. As we do battle with the Demons of Disquiet, it is easy for our ruminations to go astray. We forget to stop and think about what we are dwelling on. We don't feel like asking whose voice we are listening to. We are too tired to adjust to God's truth. We don't have the strength to reframe. We forget to remember.

This is why we need regular and sustained periods of prayer and meditation with God. We need our souls to be reset. We need to revisit God's truth over and over again so it gets deep in our bones. We need the deep rest that meditating on God's Word, God's work, and God's ways provides. We need to declutter ourselves from the chaos of life so we can enter each day with a refreshed soul.

In appendix C, I offer a pattern for our daily meditations. This begins by removing physical distractions, particularly electronic ones. It continues by asking God's Spirit to lead us through three stages: cleansing, decluttering, and communing. For me, this process has transformed my ability to discipline my ruminations and do battle with the Demons of Disquiet.

As we coach ourselves through the process of retraining our thoughts, we can recover—or discover for the first time—our true identity and God's. We can begin to see ourselves for who he declares us to be. We can realize The God of Our Circumstances knows what he's doing and ultimately has our best interest in mind. We can begin the journey toward quieter souls.

But it still might involve some pain.

QUESTIONS FOR REFLECTION AND DISCUSSION

1. Think about the way you frame your reality. Can you provide examples when your framing of reality led you to wrong conclusions? Why do we need to constantly reframe reality through spiritual lenses?

2. Why is it so hard for us to believe that God knows what he's doing and that he has our best interest in mind? How can intellectual belief fail to translate into "real life" belief?

3. Why is the habit of remembering so important for the Christian? What practices do you follow to "remember to remember"? If you don't currently make this a habit, are you willing to start?

4. Do you use regular meditation with God to cleanse the palate of your soul? If not, how could using appendix C as a guide help you form new habits?

CHAPTER 11

RECOVERING A HEART
OF TRUST

"It builds character."
During my years at the Air Force Academy, we threw that phrase around whenever we had to endure some discipline we wished we could avoid. It was our snarky response to a military regimen that was rarely fun.

Fast-forward to graduation day, when a thousand hats flew into the air and the mood was much more celebratory. Everybody was happy to be done, and I doubt one person wished that the experience had been easier. Now that the hardship was in the rearview mirror, it made the joy of completion that much sweeter.

So it is with most of the trials of life. We will do anything possible to avoid them. We often go through them embittered, jaded, and angry. But after we pass through and reflect on them, they often yield an unexpected purpose.

We sometimes find ourselves saying, "That was painful, but I needed to experience it because it prepared me for . . ."

That's certainly the case when God is behind the trial.

The Tension of Trust

Anyone who has ever formed a relationship with another person knows the tension of trust. Trust is essential. We all know that if we can't trust the other person—if we don't believe they can and will do what they say—the relationship is doomed. But we've been hurt. Lots of painful things have happened since we were little children looking up into our parents' eyes, believing everything they told us. We've been wounded. We've wounded others.

It's hard to trust others. *It's hard to trust ourselves.*

Yet every honest analysis of the disquieted soul comes down to the conclusion that we must learn to recover a heart of trust. We must learn to look into God's eyes the way we first looked into our parents'. Many teachers make the mistake of jumping right to trust, without first tackling the spadework of our identity and The God of Our Circumstances. Nevertheless, here we are at the conclusion. We eventually get to trust.

Not surprisingly, recovering a heart of trust is also a spiritual discipline. It involves more circuit training. Specifically, it involves marinating in three truths:

- God is honest about our trials.
- There is purpose for our pain.
- God is wearing our wounds.

In This World, You Will Have Troubles

When determining whether someone is trustworthy, the most important thing to know is whether they are honest. Will they tell us the truth? Are their words and actions marked by integrity? When it comes to the issue of trials and pain, God is just that.

If we want to know whether we're dealing with a Christian snake-oil salesperson, we can listen to how many times they offer a life of comfort and ease. Jesus did not. When he told us, "In this world you will have trouble" (John 16:33), he was being brutally honest. While life can overflow with happy memories, its trail is also one of tears. Jesus knew that. He personally experienced it. He did not sugarcoat the reality of pain and sorrow; he told us to expect it.

But the truth about trouble is sandwiched between two other truths: "I have told you these things, so that in me you may have peace . . . Take heart! I have overcome the world" (John 16:33). Trials may come, but if we are in Christ, our elder brother has lived them—and lives ours alongside us.

Of course the disquieted soul has a hard time believing this. Disquiet thinks it can control away trouble and escape from pain—or turn to a Cruel Master to help it cope. Knowingly or not, the disquieted soul has bought into the gospel of our culture. It's a gospel grounded in a highly internal locus of control and a relatively high level of comfort. It teaches us that trouble and pain should not be part of our lives. We should not expect them. We should do anything to avoid them.

Jesus says this belief is false. And Peter, one of the Bible's most disquieted souls, reminds us, "Dear friends, do not be surprised at the fiery ordeal that has come on you to test you, as though something strange were happening to you" (1 Peter 4:12). Similarly, James tells us, "Consider it pure joy…whenever you face trials of many kinds, because you know that the testing of your faith produces perseverance" (James 1:2).

In other words, expect hardship. Prepare for it. Don't try to bypass it. Because, although it is not always easy to see, The God of Our Circumstances is using hardship to prepare us. We can't be at the Waffle House when we need to be at the gym. The resulting physical exam will not go so well.

God is not being arbitrary and capricious; there is purpose in our pain.

Purpose in Our Pain

Most of us get the idea of no pain, no gain. We understand people who are willing to toil and sacrifice for a goal. We see athletes endlessly punishing themselves to achieve a title.

We see artists committing thousands of hours to master their craft. We know they have a love for their endeavor, but we also know there's a tremendous amount of sacrifice—and pain.

What makes the pain of ordinary life so different? Why will we voluntarily enter into pain on one hand but stay as far away from it as possible on the other? According to motivational theory, the answer is simple: We are willing to sacrifice for the pursuit of a goal that we value.

With God pain always serves a purpose, but it's not always easy to see. Hebrews 12:11 tells us, "No discipline seems pleasant at the time, but painful. Later on, however, it produces a harvest of righteousness and peace for those who have been trained by it." The general principle makes sense. We understand pain now for a prize later. The problem is, God doesn't offer us a visible sports trophy, cheering fan base, or fat contract for which to compete. Obtaining righteousness and peace is a fuzzy goal. Our crowns in heaven seem distant. It's easy to lose our motivation.

That's why we need to keep the big picture when we're in the midst of trials and suffering—or when we're tempted to avoid them. We need to get back to the disciplines of reframing and remembering. We need to reframe our reality of what suffering actually produces in us. We need to reflect on how our own trials make us wiser, more compassionate, more empathetic, and more able to speak personally to those struggling in their own pain. We need to remember people like Joseph who lived in a prison cell—unfairly slandered for doing good—so he might be in the right place at the right time to save his entire nation. I suspect that every person who is in Christ and has experienced deep pain looks back on it and says, "I understand now why God had me go through that." But it's easy to forget.

When he tells us to "consider it pure joy when you encounter trials of many kinds," James reminds us that there's joy as well as purpose in the pain. *But the joy isn't the trial.* The joy is knowing there will be a graduation day when our hats fly into the air and we can say it was all worth it. If we don't reframe and remember that truth, we will go back to trying to control the pain away or turn it over to a Cruel Master.

The rearview mirror is a wonderful thing. The trick is to remember that truth when we are staring at the windshield—and to remember who went there first.

Wearing Our Wounds

In his book *Long Journey Home*, Os Guinness recounts an event witnessed by Baroness Caroline Cox, the CEO of Humanitarian Aid Relief and member of the UK parliament. Cox tells of a brutal raid of a Dinka village in Sudan, where government soldiers butchered over one hundred men, devastated the village, and carried many more adults and children away into slavery. Cox described the human genocide as the "worst moment" in her many years of humanitarian relief.

Then she described her "best moment." Guinness writes:

> With the raiders gone and the results of their cruelty all around—husbands slain, children kidnapped into slavery, homes ruined, and they themselves brutally raped—the few women still alive were pulling themselves together. Their first instinctive act was to make tiny crosses out of sticks lying on the ground and to push them into the earth.
>
> What were they doing? Fashioning instant memorials to those they had lost? No, Lady Cox explained, the crudely formed crosses were not grave markers but symbols. The crossed sticks, pressed into the ground at the moment when their bodies reeled and their hearts bled, were acts of faith. As followers of Jesus of Nazareth, they served a God whom they believed knew pain as they knew pain. Blinded by pain and grief themselves, horribly aware the world would neither know nor care about their plight, they still staked out their lives on the conviction that there was one who knew and cared. They were not alone.[1]

These women suffered the type of human cruelty we naturally do anything to avoid. It is also the type of cruelty that leads many to reject the Christian God. So why did these women not only accept the Christian God but run to him in this moment of savagery?

Because God himself wore their wounds. And, as Guinness states, *no other God has wounds*.

People will not trust leaders who ask their followers to do something they won't. Leadership by example—or from the front, as it is often called—is the topic of endless books and articles. And as many have noted, Jesus leads from the front.

When Jesus came into this world, he entered into and through pain. As he left the world, he left through pain. He was a man of suffering, familiar with deepest grief. He took up our pain and bore our suffering. The punishment that brought us peace was on him, and by *his wounds* we are healed. Wherever we may go, he has already gone. Therefore, as the writer of Hebrews tells us, we have a God who empathizes with our weaknesses. He went through our trials before we did.

Yet the same Jesus who leads from the front also journeys alongside. This is what the Dinka women knew. Even in their deepest sadness, they were accompanied by the One who also had experienced the deepest sadness. Despite the savagery of their circumstances, he lived through it with them. Though they walked through the valley of the shadow of death, he journeyed with them—step by step and tear by tear. *He was with them*. They were not alone.

This is the paradox of pain. When we are willing to enter into pain, we can find peace in the One who went there first—and goes there again with us. We find a gateway into communion with the One who wears our wounds and heals our souls. This truth is counterintuitive. This communion is inexpressible. But it is true.

Once we realize that, we have a genuine reason to trust.

QUESTIONS FOR REFLECTION AND DISCUSSION

1. Why is it so hard to trust? Why is trust essential for curing our soul's disquiet?

2. What control techniques do you use to avoid hardship? Do you believe the statement, "When we try to shield ourselves from pain and always try to counter or avoid the next threat, it only brings more misery?"

3. What is God's purpose in our pain? Write down instances in your life when you said, "Now I understand now why God had me go through that." Why is it so easy to forget those instances?

4. What does it mean to you that Jesus wears your wounds and journeys through your pain? Why is this important when it comes to trusting God?

CHAPTER 12

QUIETING OUR SOULS

Quiet—a state of subdued calm, stillness, and peace.

My soul, be quiet before God,
for from him comes my hope (Psalm 62:5 ESV)

In a sermon related to this verse, Alistair Begg paints a picture of a young child alone in a room, huddled in a little chair. The child has recently experienced some painful suffering and is still crying audibly. As we walk through the door, we hear the child shuddering in an effort to regain control. We speak but the child can only muster short, quivering responses. Their breathing is uneven and shaky. The eyes are red and bloodshot. But slowly and surely, the wavering breathing begins to subside. The tears cease flowing. The voice begins to calm. The quivering ceases.[1]

They are quieting their soul.

We have all experienced this scene—as parents, children, or both. We know what it feels like. So we know what David means when he coaches his soul to be quiet. We know how to calm ourselves.

Thought Patterns

If calming a persistently disquieted soul was as simple as calming the little child in the chair, we would certainly not need a book about it. But as the illustration shows, and as I stated in chapter 9, this scene can be our starting point. We know how to speak to ourselves. We know how to harness our thoughts and emotions, albeit imperfectly. We understand self-discipline and self-direction, even to a small degree. That's where we begin.

I recently attended an active shooter training course. It was lecture based, and we didn't move around much. But the instructor encouraged us to think through the process of how we would respond to various shooting threats. He took us through different scenarios and different physical locations, asking us to think through our responses over and over again. His message was simple: the body won't go where the mind has never been. Similarly, if we want to begin restraining our disquieted souls, our thoughts needs to take the lead.

Rumination has been my refrain for the last several chapters. Now we can pull the path of deliverance together into a single, integrated chain:

Stop and Think—Ask—Adjust—Reframe—Remember—Trust

> *Stop and Think*—What am I dwelling on? Where is my mind taking me at this very moment? What am I mentally chewing on?

Ask—Whose voice am I hearing? Is it a voice of shame or pride? Is it falsely condemning me? Is it falsely comparing and congratulating me?

Adjust—Adjust to God's truth, not my own. Listen to his voice about who I am and my circumstances. Who does he say that I am? What is his voice telling me?

Reframe—Reframe my reality. Ask to see him in the circumstances of life. Ask for spiritual eyes, not just physical ones. Ask to see life from his perspective, not just my own.

Remember—He knows what he's doing, and he is working in the minutest details of life. He knows what I need, and he has things under control. Things will work out exactly as they should; he's come through before.

Trust—He has been honest about the troubles of life; there is purpose in any pain I experience. He is wearing my wounds. He has gone before me and he is going with me. He is trustworthy.

Again, I emphasize this is not a chant or a mantra. These are not magic words with special powers. They simply provide a way to organize our thoughts. They figuratively, and perhaps even literally, carve out new neural pathways. They encourage active meditation. They setup our circuit training regimen.

Circuit Training

Throughout this book I've intentionally used physical training as an analogy for spiritual discipline. The apostle Paul does the same in 1 Corinthians 9 and 2 Timothy 2. While we acknowledge that physical training itself is only of some value (1 Timothy 4:8), its underlying principles nicely parallel spiritual training.

The following circuit training map helps us visually remember the path of deliverance.

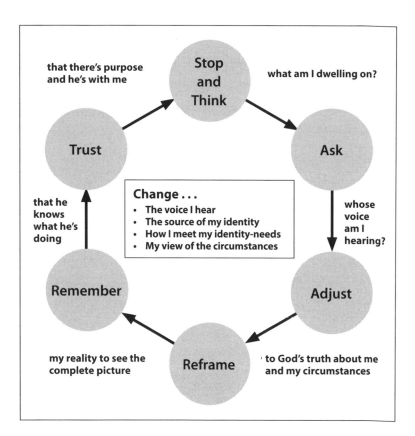

The circuit training concept is particularly apropos because the process is circular and recurring. To some degree, each station stands on its own in the exercise cycle. Each station has a unique purpose. Yet the stations work together to accomplish our collective paradigm shift. The path to deliverance from a disquieted soul is best seen as a *regular and recurring discipline* of spiritual circuit training. It's a training regimen we never graduate from.

But one huge difference separates this spiritual circuit training from our physical fitness routine. Our horsepower comes entirely from God.

Faith Acts Reliantly

Not many years ago I would have rejected the idea of spiritual circuit training outright. First, I would have convinced myself I didn't need it because I had everything under control. Spiritual discipline was for those who needed help—and I didn't need help. Second, I would have suggested it smacked of works-based righteousness. It smelled a lot like legalism.

If you have read this book and side with my first premise, I can only say, from my own experience, that God radically changed my perspective. As self-sufficient as I thought I was, God showed me a different reality about myself and my own limitations that I hope I never forget.

For those in the second camp, I offer an alternative theological perspective, with the proposed moniker Faith Acts Reliantly. In my experience, if we don't maintain this balance in our spiritual development, we won't get "F.A.R."

The earliest Protestant reformers shared a phrase that essentially stated, "There is a faith alone that justifies, and yet the faith that justifies is not alone."[2] Sometimes this is shortened to, "We are saved by faith alone, but not by a faith that is alone." Either way, this beautiful equilibrium is captured when we compare Philippians 2:12 ("continue to work out your salvation with fear and trembling") with Philippians 2:13 ("for it is God who works in you to will and to act according to his good purpose").

In other words, our faith *acts*. Faith is not sedentary. Faith gets off the couch. Faith goes to the spiritual weight room. But our faith also *relies*. Faith does not depend on its abilities nor its own power. In other words, Faith Acts Reliantly.

This truth is also highlighted in passive imperative passages like 2 Timothy 2:1, where, the apostle Paul tells Timothy to be strong. That's an imperative command. It requires action. It means, hit the weight room. But Paul counters with, "in the grace that is in Christ Jesus." In other words, apart from Christ's grace and strength we won't have the energy to walk into the weight room, let alone use it.

So Faith Acts and Faith Relies. Faith Acts Reliantly. Spiritual discipline, when undertaken with this balanced perspective, is not only acceptable—it is essential.

Growing Quieter

Most days I drive across Florida's Intracoastal Waterway. On many of those days, I see a powerful yet fairly calm river—restful and peaceful as the sun charts a path over its banks. The water is balanced and tranquil. It is often serene and still. It is majestically at ease.

Yet on other days, when a gale blows over the same river, its waters are restless and turbulent. It churns and spills over the banks. For a time, it lives in a state of disturbance, buffeting everyone and everything that comes in its path.

So it is with my restored soul. It is a soul that is increasingly quieted and stilled before God. It is a soul that has seen the path of deliverance take form. Yet, as I wrote at the beginning of this book:

> Full deliverance for the disquieted soul will never come in this lifetime. The soul's disquiet ultimately stems from a haunting desire to recover paradise lost. Despite its frequent ugliness, the disquieted soul instinctively knows that a perfect lover, perfect peace, and perfect satisfaction truly exist—but it fails in its vain attempts to find them in this world. Many quote Augustine's confession, "our hearts are restless until they rest in you." But no heart finds complete rest this side of eternity.

This is still true. The path of deliverance for our soul's disquiet is no silver bullet. Yet I have offered some hope that, even on this side of the chasm, we can do better than incessant disquiet. We can know more balance and tranquility, even in the midst of life's demands. We can trace through life's high and low tides, while remaining increasingly stable in their midst. We can increasingly live within the disharmony of life without being enslaved to that disharmony.

We can learn—and relearn—to quiet our souls.

QUESTIONS FOR REFLECTION AND DISCUSSION

1. Reflect on the chain: Stop and Think—Ask—Adjust—Reframe—Remember—Trust. Commit it to memory. Rehearse the questions and statements in the circuit training diagram.

2. Will you commit yourself to practice daily meditation (appendix C) and spiritual circuit training for 30 days? Will you ask God for strength to stick with it and make it a habit?

3. If you find that this recurring practice of meditation and spiritual circuit training begins to quiet your soul, will you share it with another person struggling with disquiet?

CONCLUSION

There's a saying in my old line of work that it's time to shoot the engineers. That is, we've spent enough time designing, redesigning, and tinkering. It's time to build the product.

That concept can ring true in Christian circles as well. We who are given to introspection can spend a lifetime fixing ourselves and never get around to doing the hard business of the kingdom. There's a very real risk of spending too much time in therapy.

On the other hand, many people try to live life like an athlete playing with a torn ACL. Our society can be a breeding ground for disquiet in its many forms. We often need to undergo spiritual surgery before we can truly be effective on the court.

Quieter souls are freer souls. Those unburdened from nonstop attacks of shame and guilt are able to give more freely of themselves. Quieter souls know who God says they are and how their identity-needs can be met. They, in turn, are able to help others do the same. Quieter souls can see life's circumstances in a much more hopeful way, because they know The God of Our Circumstances. And they are able to pass that confidence and hope on to others. Quieter souls are more contented souls—less anxious, worried, and scared. The world could use a lot more of that.

In short, quieter souls have more of their life and love to give away.

Let's do that together.

SHAME

Adam and his wife were both naked, and they felt no shame. (Genesis 2:25)

Then the eyes of both of them were opened, and they realized they were naked; so they sewed fig leaves together and made coverings for themselves. (Genesis 3:7)

The watershed moment between these two passages was mankind's original sin against God. The Bible clearly tells us that shame was the most immediate and recognizable consequence of the fall. It also tells us that shame immediately evokes a sense of nakedness and exposure, causing us to want to want to cover up and hide. In fact, the Proto-Indo-European root *skem* ("shame") literally means "to cover, to veil, to hide." [1]

Shame is the humiliation we feel when we are personally ridiculed, scorned, and rejected. For example, reflect on your feelings when you hear the following statements:

- You are disgusting.
- You are a complete failure.
- You are totally worthless.
- You are a disgrace.
- You are a complete disappointment.
- You are a total reject.
- Why would anyone want to be with you?
- You mean nothing to me.
- You should just die.

These are extremely strong statements of condemnation, and some people may hear this chorus quite loudly. Others may hear a slightly different one:

- You're not good enough.
- You don't count.
- You bring nothing to the table.
- You don't really matter.
- You won't ever amount to much.
- You're ugly.
- You're not lovely.
- No one really cares about you.

To the degree we personally identify with either of these types of statements, we are impacted by the voice of shame. Not everyone is equally affected. Both nature and nurture combine to influence everyone differently. But to some degree we all feel shame's condemnation, and it reinforces what we tend to already believe about ourselves.

As I discuss in chapter 7, shame's condemnation is exactly what Jesus came to overcome. But unless we understand the power and pathology of shame, we may not understand how deeply rooted it is, even lurking in the depths of our subconscious.

Shame and Guilt

Let's return to the previous statements of shame. Consider what these statements are not saying. They are *not* saying:

I hurt you and I apologize for that.
I wronged you and I want to make it right.
I sinned against you; please forgive me.

These statements are normal, healthy statements stemming from our self-awareness of a wrongdoing and a desire to correct it. While the wrongdoing might be performance-related, such as a mistake at work, such wrongdoing is normally centered on harm we have caused another person. We missed the mark and we need to make amends.

Some behaviorists call this "good shame." However, I prefer the term guilt. As Brené Brown states, "Shame is a focus on self, guilt is a focus on behavior. Shame is 'I am bad.' Guilt is 'I did something bad.'"[2] Guilt is the natural consequence of failing to meet a necessary standard and, while we may be overly guilt ridden, guilt is normally a healthy response that leads to a desire for repentance and restoration. As some have noted, the absence of guilt—particularly over how we treat others—is a clear mark of psychopathy.

Shame, on the other hand, has few, if any, truly redemptive benefits. The humiliation of shame can be a strong motivator, but it typically leads to unhealthy behavior. For example, during my four years of military high school, I never received a single demerit—a rare feat. But I had incentive: The names of those who had been "written up" were publicly announced before the entire corps of cadets each morning. Those who had received demerits had to walk tours in the quadrangle for everyone to see. It was public shaming. To the degree that it discouraged bad external behavior, it was *very* effective.

However, as in all kinds of honor-shame cultures, this shame-based motivation ultimately yields unhealthy internal results. As I discuss in chapter 2, the Demons of Disquiet feast on our shame avoidance. Obsessive behaviors, perfectionism, and Cruel Masters of all sorts spawn from our desire to control away shame's effects. Shame avoidance can yield effective external behavior modification. But internally we just learn to hide—or disappear altogether.

As the Bible shows us, shame always hides—and sometimes it hides in *pride*.

Shame and Pride

Throughout the book, I treat shame and pride as opposite extremes. As stated in chapter 1:

Shame feels inferior while pride feels superior. Shame hears voices of disapproval, while pride hears voices of applause. Shame defensively hides in the shadows. Pride bombastically parades in the streets.

However, shame and pride are not as unrelated as they may seem. In fact, for some of us, pride is often, if not always, just another mask to cover our shame and to expose another's.

To help understand this, we might reflect on C. S. Lewis's penetrating observations regarding pride. In *Mere Christianity* Lewis writes:

I pointed out a moment ago that the more pride one had, the more one disliked pride in others. In fact, if you want to find out how proud you are the easiest way is to ask yourself, "How much do I dislike it when other people snub me, or refuse to take any notice of me, or shove their oar in, or patronize me, or show off?" The point is that each person's pride is in competition with everyone else's pride. It is because I wanted to be the big noise at the party that I am so annoyed at someone else being the big noise. Two of a trade never agree.[3]

He continues, regarding the competitive nature of pride:

Pride gets no pleasure out of having something, only out of having more of it than the next man. We say that people are proud of being rich, or clever, or good-looking, but they are not. They are proud of being richer, or cleverer, or better-looking than others. If everyone else became equally rich, or clever, or good-looking there would be nothing to be proud about. It is the comparison that makes you proud: the pleasure of being above the rest. Once the element of competition has gone, pride has gone.[4]

This is a valuable and insightful observation. But the ultimate question is, why is it true? Why are we annoyed at others' showing off in areas in which we excel? Why are billionaires agitated over the success of other billionaires? I've observed it is because *someone else's pride penetrates our shame.* Someone performing better than us, particularly in areas we excel in, makes us feel like worthless, disgraceful, disappointing, and rejected nobodies.

This is the cycle of shame and pride that can lie at the root of our personal conflict—and our disquiet.

I am not the first to suggest this cyclical relationship. In her review of *The City of God*, Stephanie Arel notes the Augustinian belief that human pride is the origin of the "evil will" that preceded mankind's first sin. This self-worshiping pride resulted in shame, which was the penalty for pride's false exaltation. However, she also notes Augustine's position that after the fall, "pride hides shame in the first place."[5]

Therefore, when we pull back the covers, shame and pride may be so inextricably linked in some of us that one never appears without the other. "Which came first" may be debated by the experts. But whatever the conclusion, I am convinced of this: The common denominator of both shame and pride is a *deformed sense of self.*

And that is what Jesus came to make new.

WHAT IS THE GOSPEL?

While many different summaries of the Christian gospel exist, I offer the following:

The gospel is the *good news* that, through Jesus Christ, God made a way to *redeem* us from death and *reconcile* us to himself, so that we might have an eternal *relationship* with him.

I'll briefly discuss each of these key themes.

Good News — The word "gospel" or "good spell" is a rendering of the Greek word *evangelion*, which means "good news" or "good message." In Romans 1 Paul writes that he is not ashamed of the gospel because it is the power of God for salvation for everyone who believes. This is truly good news because the way out of spiritual death and into new and everlasting life with God is the best message that anyone could ever receive.

Redemption — In Ephesians 1:7 Paul writes, "In [Christ] we have redemption through his blood, the forgiveness of sins, in accordance with the riches of God's grace." "Redeem" means to buy something back. It conveys the essential truth that, through Jesus Christ, God has bought us back from eternal death, which is the penalty for our sin. The essence of redemption is that on the cross Jesus provided his life as a ransom to purchase ours and that his perfect life is the only life valuable enough to conduct that purchase. He delivered us from our sin and death by providing the bride price needed for our wedding day with God.

Reconciliation — In Colossians 1:21, Paul tells us that our evil behavior alienated us from God, making us his enemies. Like a cracked mirror, we bear the remnants of God's image, but we are far too distorted to be united with him on our own. Jesus came to deal with that. As a friend of sinners, he reconciles us to God by providing the perfect substitution. This substitution is described in 2 Corinthians 5:21: "God made him who had no sin to be sin for us, so that in him we might become the righteousness of God." It is only through this transaction that we, who are outsiders, may have peace with God and be reconciled to him. Apart from Christ we are aliens and enemies of God. In Christ we are children adopted into God's family. We are the wayward who have found our way home. In ourselves we were lost. In him we are found.

Relationship — The beauty of the gospel is that we are not just saved *from* something; we are saved *to* something, and that something is an eternity living in fellowship with God. It is what Jesus called eternal life, gained through the power of his resurrection from the dead. And as the term implies, this life doesn't just live in yesterday or wait for tomorrow—it beckons today. As the "mustard seed" of the relationship takes root, like any healthy relationship does, it begins to permeate every area of our lives. The gospel isn't something we *believed*; it is something we *believe*. And the gospel isn't just about something that once *happened* in our lives. The gospel is about something that is forever *happening* in our lives.

CHRISTIAN MEDITATION

Most of my encouragement for quieting our souls begins with developing radical changes in our thought patterns or ruminations. These changes come through disciplining our minds and redirecting our reflections. This process involves *active meditation*. While in our modern times meditation is largely associated with Far Eastern and New Age philosophies, it has been an essential spiritual discipline within Christianity for centuries— amongst groups as diverse as the Desert Fathers and the Puritans. Our modern tendency to abandon meditation as a spiritual discipline could directly correlate with our inability to get biblical truth from "our heads to our hearts to our hands." As Dallas Willard states:

> Disciplines are activities that *are* in our power and that enable us to do what we cannot do by direct effort. We cannot transform our ideas or images,

or even the information we have or our thought processes, into Christlikeness by direct effort. But we can do things—adopt practices—that, indirectly, will increasingly have that effect.[1]

As a spiritual discipline, Christian meditation enables just that.

Christian Meditation Defined

It is often helpful to see biblical terms defined in their original language and in the context of their usage throughout Scripture. In the case of the Hebrew Old Testament, two words for meditation are dominant: *hâgâh* and *sîychâh*, as shown.

Hebrew	Definition	Biblical Examples
hâgâh[2] haw-gaw	to murmur (in pleasure or anger); by implication, to ponder: imagine, meditate, mourn, mutter, roar, sore, speak, study, talk, utter	**Joshua 1:8** — Keep this Book of the Law always on your lips; meditate on it day and night, so that you may be careful to do everything written in it. Then you will be prosperous and successful. **Psalm 1:2** — Whose delight is in the law of the LORD, and who meditates on his law day and night. **Psalm 77:12** — I will consider all your works and meditate on all your mighty deeds. **Psalm 143:5** — I remember the days of long ago; I meditate on all your works and consider what your hands have done.

śîychâh³ see-khaw	to ponder, i.e. (by implication) converse (with oneself, and, hence, aloud) or (transitively) utter: commune, complain, declare, meditate, muse, pray, speak, talk (with)	**Psalm 119:15** — I meditate on your precepts and consider your ways. **Psalm 119:23** — Though rulers sit together and slander me, your servant will meditate on your decrees. **Psalm 119:27** — Cause me to understand the way of your precepts, that I may meditate on your wonderful deeds. **Psalm 119:48** — I reach out for your commands, which I love, that I may meditate on your decrees.

Some common themes link both of these words. First, the process involves high levels of mental engagement. Some scholars call biblical meditation the act of "mental chewing." That is, meditation involves extensive pondering, musing, and even verbalization. Joyce Meyer commented, "If you know how to worry, you know how to meditate,"⁴ because they involve the same process (albeit to different outcomes), of playing and replaying our thoughts. Meditation can also involve actively speaking through our period of reflection.

Finally, we should note the common objects of biblical meditation, which are *God's Word, his work,* and *his ways.* Not surprisingly, meditation is often connected with prayer. Charles Spurgeon observed, "Meditation and prayer are twin sisters, and both of them appear to me equally necessary to a Christian life. I think meditation must exist where there is prayer, and prayer would be sure to exist where there is meditation."[5]

In the case of the Greek New Testament, two words may be applied to meditation: *meletaō* and, to a lesser extent, *logizomai*.

Greek	Definition	Biblical Examples
meletaō[6] mel-et-ah'-o	to take care of, i.e., (by implication) revolve in the mind: imagine, premeditate	**Acts 4:25** — "You spoke by the Holy Spirit through the mouth of your servant, our father David: 'Why do the nations rage and the peoples plot in vain?'"
		1 Timothy 4:15 — Be diligent in these matters; give yourself wholly to them, so that everyone may see your progress.
logizomai[7] log-id'-zom-ahee	to take an inventory, i.e., estimate (literally or figuratively): conclude, (ac-)count (of), despise, esteem, impute, lay, number, reason, reckon, suppose, think (on)	**Philippians 4:8** — Finally, brothers and sisters, whatever is true, whatever is noble, whatever is right, whatever is pure, whatever is lovely, whatever is admirable—if anything is excellent or praiseworthy— think about such things.

Meletaō, "revolving in the mind," reinforces the idea of playing and replaying our thoughts. While the "plotting in vain" of Acts 4:25 is not the type of biblical meditation we pursue, the *process* is the same. Plotting, or premeditation, involves active thinking, over and over again, on a specific object or outcome. Similarly, *logizomai,* in the context of Philippians 4:8, exhorts us to "think on" true, noble, right, pure, lovely, admirable, excellent, and praiseworthy things. Colossians 3:2, likewise, encourages us to "set [our] minds on things above." This practice does not imply a single event; rather it suggests recurrence—like a revolving door—where we continually return our minds to the objects of our meditations.

Finally, Christian meditation involves more than physical brain exercise; it consists of aligning our mental and spiritual gaze with God and his truth. When the Bible speaks of setting our minds on things above, it is not simply speaking of directing our physical brain waves. Rather, it is an encouragement to focus our physical and spiritual selves on heavenly things. To aid us, we invoke or summon God's Spirit to "guide [us] into all truth" (John 16:13). Thus, while Christian and Far Eastern meditation may both quietly and reflectively concentrate, Christian meditation does not encourage us to clear or empty ourselves. Rather, Christian meditation propels us to *fill ourselves,* invoking God's Spirit to direct our recurring thoughts toward God's Word, work, and ways—which are primarily found in Scripture itself.

What Does Christian Meditation Achieve?

Psalm 104 is a beautiful psalm of meditation. It provides what Charles Spurgeon refers to as "one of the loftiest and longest sustained flights of the inspired muse." Spurgeon writes:

> The psalm gives an interpretation to the many voices of nature, and sings sweetly both of creation and providence. The poem contains a complete cosmos: sea and land, cloud and sunlight, plant and animal, light and darkness, life and death are all proved to be expressive of the presence of the Lord.[8]

At the psalm's conclusion, David the psalmist writes, "May my meditation be pleasing to him as I rejoice in the LORD" (v. 34). This is our chief end—that our meditations would be pleasing to him or, in the words of Psalm 141:2, "set before [him] like incense." Meditation itself is an act of worship that glorifies God.

But biblical meditation also unlocks the door to the spiritual circuit training discussed throughout this book. It is essential for retraining the ruminations of the disquieted soul. Returning to Spurgeon,

> Meditation is the *machine in which the raw material of knowledge is converted to the best uses*. Let me compare it to a wine-press. By reading, and research,

and study we gather the grapes; but it is by meditation we press out the juice of those grapes, and obtain the wine.[9]

This conversion of grapes to wine is, to borrow from chapter 7, analogous to getting God's truth *deep in our bones*. A phrase attributed to a few sources essentially states, "A thought becomes a word. A word becomes an action. An action becomes a habit. A habit becomes your character." Meditation is a central link from thought to character.

To see this played out, we only need to consider pornography. If we watch pornographic material, it invites the active meditations of our minds, which revolve—over and again—around those images. This stimulates physical response, but it doesn't end there. The images return to our minds and our minds further dwell (meditate) on them. This invites the use of more visualization, more physical response, and an eventual habit that grows to affect our entire character.

This concept is the same when applied to right uses, except that it is harder to train ourselves to meditate on God's Word, work, and ways than it is to meditate on pornography, worry, bitterness, or any other negative mental chewing. That is why we must come back to *invoking God's Spirit* in the process—we are simply too weak in ourselves to practice lofty meditations without God's consistent assistance.

Finally, while the primary benefit of Christian meditation consists of getting God's truth deep in our bones, an added

provision is what Spurgeon calls, "the couch of the soul."
That is, meditation actually furnishes the mind with *rest*.
Spurgeon states, "If many of us knew how to spend a little
time daily in the calm repose of contemplative retirement,
we should find ourselves less exhausted by the wear and tear
of our worldly duties."[10]

The idea of meditation as rest might seem unusual, given
that, as I have defined it, meditation involves the active
discipline of our thoughts. Rest, in its modern definition,
translates to passivity—like sitting idly in a chair with a
drink in our hand, zoned out in front of a screen. While this
is certainly *inactive*, in my experience it is not ultimately as
restful as training ourselves to change our mental posture,
broaden the expanses of our minds, and refocus our
preoccupations. So much mental churning and angst can
be released by simply reflecting on the vastness of a starry
night, the rhythm of ocean waves, or any majestic picture
of God and his creation. How small and insignificant our
problems become when we paint them against the backdrop
of creation and the Creator's splendor.

How Should the Christian Meditate?

For most of my adult life, I have been visited by bouts of
insomnia. I wake up around 2 a.m. and stay awake for one
to two hours. The cycle is like clockwork.

For many years I used that window of time to get on the
computer and work. However, when I found that habit left me

irritable throughout the day, I began forcing myself to lie still and mentally recite all the verses from Scripture that came to mind, until I fell asleep again. It was a rather unorganized process—perhaps a spiritual version of counting sheep—but I came to enjoy God's calming presence during those times. He often used the time to relax my soul.

What I didn't know was that I was haphazardly applying a few basic principles of Christian meditation. I tell this story, not because it is a great example to follow, but to highlight meditation's most important ingredient: *intentional practice*. Meditation needn't be formulaic or ritualistic—and it certainly won't feel perfect—but it should be intentional and disciplined. This requires self-coaching.

In his book *Spiritual Depression* Martin Lloyd-Jones states that the main trouble with our soul's disquiet is that we "allow ourselves to talk to us instead of talking to ourselves." At first glance this statement may seem puzzling. However, referencing Psalm 42, he explains:

Am I just trying to be deliberately paradoxical? Far from it . . . Take those thoughts that come to you the moment you wake up in the morning. You have not originated them, but they start talking to you, they bring back the problems of yesterday, etc. Someone is talking. Who is talking to you? Your self is talking to you. Now [the psalmist's] treatment was this; instead of allowing this self to talk to him, he starts talking to himself. "Why art thou cast down, O my soul?" he asks. His soul has been depressing him, crushing him. So he stands up and says: "Self, listen for a moment, I will speak to you." [11]

Lloyd-Jones is describing the self-coaching I have noted in part II of this book. Like its use when controlling our daily ruminations, self-coaching is also the process we must use when practicing regular meditation. Otherwise, our minds wander, our thoughts become distracted, we begin staring at our electronic devices, and our communion is broken.

To avoid this, we must *coach ourselves* through the entire process. We begin by developing a recurring time for meditation, during which we intentionally remove all elements of distraction. We need to put the electronic gadgets in another place and center our thoughts on God's Word, work, and ways. Whatever place or places we may choose to meditate, they should be free from the ongoing distractions of this world.

We must also actively seek God's presence and power throughout our time of meditation. In the words of Psalm 16:11, "You will fill me with joy in your presence, with eternal pleasures at your right hand." Through meditation, we can and will experience the joy of God's presence as he leads us through three key stages: *cleansing, decluttering,* and *communing.*

"Create in me a clean heart, O God, and renew a right spirit within me" (Psalm 51:10 ESV). Scripture frequently paints this image of spiritual cleansing, which we too should adopt. Rather than simply offering God a laundry list of every sin we can recall, followed by a quick prayer for forgiveness, we should first invite God to search and "see if there is any offensive way in me" (Psalm 139:24). As he reveals the dark and often hidden stains of our sin, we may then dwell on the image of God washing our souls. David writes, "Cleanse me with hyssop, and I will be clean; wash me, and I will be whiter than snow" (Psalm 51:7). We need to enter our communion with *clean souls*.

We also need to enter our communion with *uncluttered* souls. In our noisy and frenetic world, we need to be intentional about decluttering ourselves. Our minds naturally enter into meditation full of wandering and often toxic thoughts. Richard Foster writes, "In contemporary society our Adversary majors in three things: noise, hurry, and crowds. If he can keep us engaged in 'muchness' and 'manyness,' he will rest satisfied." [12] This, of course, describes the language of disquiet, and we need God's Spirit to break through this clutter. We need our thoughts defragmented. Our souls need calming. We need the "peace of God, which transcends all understanding" (Philippians 4:7) to flood the chaotic sanctuaries of our hearts.

We often also need God to bind up our hearts. We may be entering our times of meditation as harassed and wounded people. Our hearts have been lanced by the pains of this world. We are doing mental battle with real or imagined adversaries. Along with needing calm, our hearts also need to be strengthened. We need, in the words of Thomas Watson, to "apply the medicine of Christ's blood" to our wounds. We need to recover the words of Psalm 73:26: "My flesh and my heart may fail, but God is the strength of my heart and my portion forever."

Third, we should focus on intimate *communion*. This involves the practice of both reflecting and listening. We *reflect* on who God is and, as a result, who we are. We also *listen* through God's Word and his Spirit for his leading in our lives.

This, of course, leads us to ask how we should focus our specific reflections. Stating that we should focus on God's Word, work, and ways paints with a very broad brush. The Puritans cited no less than fifty themes for meditation.[13] Spurgeon offered various attributes of the persons of the Trinity but focused particularly on the sweetness of our fellowship with Christ.[14] I might simply offer that we begin with a scriptural word and branch outward.

For example, I am currently focused on the word joy. As I meditate, I might begin by reflecting on one verse about joy, such as "restore to me the joy of your salvation" (Psalm 51:12). I might reflect on the need to regularly seek my joy in God; then I would begin to branch outward. As this branching occurs, I might recall that it was for the joy set before him that Jesus endured the cross (Hebrews 12:2). I might ask myself what that "joy set before him" means. I would then ponder Christ's joy when he redeems all his people from the ends of the earth and presents them as his gift to the Father. I could envision that wedding day of Christ and his eternal bride. I might visualize all the earth singing for joy—the rivers, fields, valleys, forests, and mountains (Psalms 96:12 and 98:8). I might see every tribe, tongue, and nation and the angels above singing, "To him who sits on the throne and to the Lamb be praise and honor and glory and power, for ever and ever!" (Revelation 5:13). I might remember that, because of that scene, I can rejoice always in the Lord. And I could say it again . . . Rejoice! (Philippians 4:4).

I would replay parts of that "mental screenplay" throughout my meditations—like a revolving door. And I would *listen*, asking God to speak to my circumstance through his Word.

This single example only touches one word and one branch. The word and the branches are nearly limitless. They could be the names of God or his many attributes. They could be the fruits of the Spirit or the excellences of Philippians 4:8. They could be the songs of his creation. *Ask God for the words and the branches.*

Christian meditation is the lost key to a door that can change the ruminations of a disquieted soul. Our meditations will often be choppy and haphazard. They will not always have the same degree of depth and inspiration. That's okay. Perfection is not required. Persistence and discipline is.

NOTES

Chapter 1

1. "A Quote by Thomas Watson," Goodreads, https://www.goodreads.com/quotes/1324168-satan-loves-to-fish-in-the-troubled-waters-of-a (accessed October 20, 2018).

2. "14 Quotes on the Forbidden," Psychology Today, January 26, 2012, https://www.psychologytoday.com/us/blog/here-there-and-everywhere/201201/14-quotes-the-forbidden (accessed October 19, 2018).

3. Augustine and Henry Chadwick. The Confessions. (New York: Oxford University Press, 1991), 3.

Chapter 2

1. Stephanie Brown, "Society's Self-Destructive Addiction to Faster Living," New York Post, January 04, 2014, https://nypost.com/2014/01/04/societys-addiction-to-faster-living-is-destroying-us-doctor/ (accessed October 19, 2018).

2. Rachel Nuwer, "Are You Addicted To Stress? Here's How To Tell," The Huffington Post, August 19, 2014, https://www.huffingtonpost.com/2014/08/19/stress-addiction_n_5689123.html (accessed October 19, 2018).

3. Christopher Ingraham, "One in Eight American Adults Is an Alcoholic, Study Says," The Washington Post, August 11, 2017, https://www.washingtonpost.com/news/wonk/wp/2017/08/11/study-one-in-eight-american-adults-are-alcoholics/?noredirect=on&utm_term=.338731936be9 (accessed October 19, 2018).

4. National Institute on Drug Abuse, "Increased Drug Availability Is Associated with Increased Use and Overdose," NIDA, https://www.drugabuse.gov/publications/research-reports/relationship-between-prescription-drug-abuse-heroin-use/increased-drug-availability-associated-increased-use-overdose (accessed October 19, 2018).

5. "Sex Addiction: Is It Common? | Sex Addiction Statistics," The Ranch. September 20,2017, https://www.recoveryranch.com/resources/sex-addiction-and-intimacy-disorders/sex-addiction-america-common/ (accessed October 19, 2018).

6. "5 Types of Behavioral Addictions Common Among Teens," Paradigm Malibu Teen Treatment Center, August 29, 2016, https://paradigmmalibu.com/5-types-of-behavioral-addictions-common-among-teens/ (accessed October 19, 2018).

7. "Process Addictions," Teen Treatment Center, 2018, https://www.teentreatmentcenter.com/teen-process-addictions/ (accessed June 27, 2018).

Chapter 3

1. Clive Staples Lewis, The Screwtape Letters (New Jersey: Revell, 1976), 53–54.

2. Lewis, Screwtape Letters, 53–54.

3. Olivia Solon, "Ex-Facebook President Sean Parker: Site Made to Exploit Human 'Vulnerability,'" The Guardian, November 09, 2017, https://www.theguardian.com/technology/2017/nov/09/facebook-sean-parker-vulnerability-brain-psychology (accessed October 19, 2018).

4. Jason A. Colquitt, Jeffery A. LePine, and Michael J. Wesson. Organizational Behavior Improving Performance and Commitment in the Workplace (New York: McGraw-Hill Education, 2019), 167–69.

5. Derek Thompson, "The 10 Things Economics Can Tell Us About Happiness," The Atlantic, May 31, 2012, https://www.theatlantic.com/business/archive/2012/05/the-10-things-economics-can-tell-us-about-happiness/257947/ (accessed October 19, 2018).

6. Jessica Gross, "6 Studies on How Money Affects the Mind," TED Blog, December 22, 2013, https://blog.ted.com/6-studies-of-money-and-the-mind/ (accessed October 19, 2018).

7. "Counterfeit Gods—Tim Keller," YouTube, April 6, 2012, https://www.youtube.com/watch?v=_mK65lpveSM&t=2084s (accessed October 19, 2018).

8. Ernest Becker, The Denial of Death (London: Souvenir Press, 2018), 167.

9. Keller, Counterfeit Gods.

Chapter 4

1. Conrad Anker, quoted in James M. Clash, "'Because it's there,'" Forbes, June 06, 2013, https://www.forbes.com/ global/2001/1029/060.html#7afdca7c2080 (accessed October 19, 2018).

2. "Type A Personality Test," Psychology Today, https://www. psychologytoday.com/us/tests/personality/type-personality-test (accessed October 19, 2018).

3. Marcus Buckingham, quoted in Bill Breen, "The Clear Leader." Fast Company. July 30, 2012, https://www.fastcompany. com/55197/clear-leader (accessed October 19, 2018).

4. Marshall Goldsmith and Mark Reiter, What Got You Here Won't Get You There: How Successful People Become Even More Successful (New York: Hachette Books, 2014), 40–41.

5. Goldsmith and Reiter, What Got You Here Won't Get You There, 17.

6. Andrew Yang, "The Dark Side of America's Achievement Culture," The Huffington Post, April 27, 2015, https:// www.huffingtonpost.com/andrewyang/the-dark-side-of-americas-achievement-culture_b_6753002.html (accessed October 19, 2018).

7. Alistair Begg, "Lessons Learned in the Valley," Truth for Life, January 8, 1995, https://www.truthforlife.org/resources/ sermon/lessons-learned-in-the-valley/ (accessed October 19, 2018).

8. Amy Simpson, "Pastors in Recovery," CT Pastors, December 28, 2015, https://www.christianitytoday.com/pastors/2016/ winter/pastors-in-recovery.html (accessed October 19, 2018).

9. Goldsmith and Reiter, What Got You Here Won't Get You, 40–41.

10. Os Guinness, Virginia Mooney, and Karen Lee-Thorp, Steering through Chaos: The Vices and Virtues in an Age of Moral Confusion (Colorado Springs: NavPress, 2000), 1–3.

11. Augustine and Henry Chadwick, The Confessions (New York: Oxford University Press, 1991), 18.

12. Peter Brown, "Dialogue With God," The New York Review of Books, October 26, 2017, https://www.nybooks.com/articles/2017/10/26/sarah-ruden-augustine-dialogue-god/ (accessed October 19, 2018).

Chapter 5

1. "9 Things Everyone Needs to Know About Depression," Core Christianity, 2018, https://corechristianity.com/resource-library/special-offers/9-things-everyone-needs-to-know-about-depression (accessed October 19, 2018).

2. "9 Things Everyone Needs to Know About Depression," Core Christianity, 2018.

3. "11 Reasons Spurgeon Was Depressed," The Spurgeon Center, July 11, 2017, https://www.spurgeon.org/resource-library/blog-entries/11-reasons-spurgeon-was-depressed (accessed October 19, 2018).

4. Ryan Griffith, "Martin Luther's Shelter Amid the Flood of Depression," The Gospel Coalition, July 6, 2017, https://www.thegospelcoalition.org/article/martin-luthers-shelter-amid-flood-of-depression/ (accessed October 19, 2018).

5. "What Causes Depression?" Harvard Health Publishing, https://www.health.harvard.edu/mind-and-mood/what-causes-depression (accessed October 19, 2018).
6. Begg, "Lessons Learned in the Valley," January 8, 1995.

Chapter 6

1. Jean-Paul Sartre, "Existentialism Is a Humanism," The Value of Knowledge, https://www.marxists.org/reference/archive/sartre/works/exist/sartre.htm (accessed October 19, 2018).
2. "The Westminster Shorter Catechism," The Westminster Presbyterian, http://www.westminsterconfession.org/confessional-standards/the-westminster-shorter-catechism.php (accessed October 19, 2018).

Chapter 7

1. Lane Cohee, Letters to Our Next Generation: Life Lessons from a Father to His Sons (CreateSpace, 2011), 20.
2. "Keynote: Tim Keller—How to Change Deeply," YouTube, June 25, 2015, https://www.youtube.com/watch?v=DQgxu Dl8DXs (accessed October 19, 2018).
3. John R. Stott, "In Christ," C. S. Lewis Institute, July 15, 2013, http://www.cslewisinstitute.org/In_Christ_page1 (accessed October 19, 2018).
4. Clive Staples Lewis, Mere Christianity (New York: HarperCollins, 2017), 122.

Chapter 8

1. Thomas S. Kuhn and Ian Hacking, The Structure of Scientific Revolutions (Chicago: University of Chicago Press, 2012).

Chapter 11

1. Os Guinness. Long Journey Home: A Guide to Your Search for the Meaning of Life (Colorado Springs: WaterBrook, 2001), 100.

Chapter 12

1. Alistair Begg. "Contentment," Truth for Life, https://www. truthforlife.org/resources/sermon/contentment/ (accessed October 19, 2018).

2. "Is Luther Really the Originator of 'We Are Saved by Faith Alone, but the Faith That Saves Is Never Alone?'" Christianity Stack Exchange, https://christianity.stackexchange.com/ questions/42366/is-luther really the originator-of-we-are-saved-by-faith-alone-but-the-faith-t (accessed October 20, 2018).

Appendix A—Shame

1. "Shame," Emotional Competency, http://www.emotional competency.com/shame.htm (accessed January 20, 2019).

2. "Brené Brown on The Difference Between Guilt and Shame," Farnam Street, January 04, 2017, https://fs.blog/2014/10/ brene-brown-guilt-shame/ (accessed January 20, 2019).

3. Lewis, Mere Christianity, 122.

4. Lewis, Mere Christianity, 122.

5. Stephanie N. Arel, Affect Theory, Shame, and Christian Formation, SpringerLink, https://link.springer.com/book/ 10.1007/978-3-319-42592-4 (accessed January 20, 2019).

Appendix C—Christian Meditation

1. Dallas Willard, Renovation of the Heart: Putting on the Character of Christ (Colorado Springs: NavPress, 2012), 113.

2. James Strong, Strong's Exhaustive Concordance of the Bible (Lynchburg, VA: Old Time Gospel Hour), 32.

3. Strong, Strong's Exhaustive Concordance of the Bible, 115.

4. "Joyce Meyer Quotes," BrainyQuote.com, BrainyMedia Inc., 2019, https://www.brainyquote.com/quotes/joyce_meyer_567530 (accessed January 20, 2019).

5. "Meditation on God by C. H. Spurgeon," Blue Letter Bible, last modified April 18, 2001, https://www.blueletterbible.org/Comm/spurgeon_charles/sermons/2690.cfm (accessed January 20, 2019).

6. Strong, Strong's Exhaustive Concordance of the Bible, 47.

7. Strong, Strong's Exhaustive Concordance of the Bible, 45.

8. Charles H. Spurgeon, "Psalm 104," The Spurgeon Archive, http://archive.spurgeon.org/treasury/ps104.php (accessed January 20, 2019).

9. "Meditation on God by C. H. Spurgeon," Blue Letter Bible.

10. "Meditation on God by C. H. Spurgeon," Blue Letter Bible.

11. David Martyn Lloyd-Jones, Spiritual Depression: Its Causes and Cure (Grand Rapids: Eerdmans, 2013), 20.

12. Richard J. Foster, Celebration of Discipline: The Path to Spiritual Growth (San Francisco: HarperOne, 2018), 22.

13. Joel R. Beeke and Mark Jones, A Puritan Theology: Doctrine for Life (Grand Rapids: Reformation Heritage Books, 2012), 899–901.

14. "Meditation on God by C. H. Spurgeon," Blue Letter Bible.

ABOUT THE AUTHOR

Lane Cohee was educated at the United States Air Force Academy, University of Redlands, University of Colorado, and Rollins College, where he received his Doctorate in Business Administration. He currently serves as an Associate Professor of Management at the Palm Beach Atlantic (PBA) University Rinker School of Business in West Palm Beach, Florida.

Prior to joining PBA, Lane spent 30 years in the defense and aerospace sector, most recently serving as an executive business leader at Harris Corporation. His instruction, research interests, and academic publications focus on organizational development, strategy, leadership, and operations, with an emphasis on project/program management. As a business practitioner, Lane served as executive committee chair for both emerging talent development and program management. He also served as an adjunct faculty instructor in the field of project management at Embry-Riddle Aeronautical University.

Lane has been an active member in congregations within the Presbyterian Church in America (PCA) since 1987. During that period, he taught over 50 courses in the areas of leadership, parenting, theology, apologetics, church history, and financial management.

Lane and Cheryl were married in 1987 and currently reside in Indialantic, Florida. They have three adult sons: Chase, Cale, and Chane.

Lane may be contacted at *lanecohee@earthlink.net*. His professional website may be accessed at *lanecohee.com*.